The Accounting Education Change Commission:

Its History and Impact

Gary L. Sundem

American Accounting Association
5717 Bessie Drive
Sarasota, FL 34233

Table of Contents

Preface   v

Chapter 1   The Climate for Change   1

Chapter 2   Formation of the Commission   5

Chapter 3   Setting the Direction   11

Chapter 4   The Grant Program   23

Chapter 5   Promoting Change   31

Chapter 6   Position and Issues Statements   39

Chapter 7   Impacts on Stakeholders   53

Chapter 8   Measuring and Assessing Change   61

Chapter 9   Conclusion   69

Appendix A   Commission Members   71

Appendix B   Perspectives on Education: Capabilities for Success in the
               Accounting Profession   87

References   97

PREFACE

What causes change? Evolutionary changes continuously affect nearly all aspects of life. But periodically, something causes a sudden change, a break in the natural evolution, maybe even a revolution. The 1990s are proving to be such a time in accounting education. This monograph examines the role of the Accounting Education Change Commission (AECC) in this revolution.

The 20 years before the appointment of the AECC were rife with suggestions for changes in accounting education, but these suggestions led to only limited actions. According to Needles and Powers (1990) there were at least 17 models for revisions in accounting education developed between 1967 and 1987, but none of them had a widespread impact.

The most significant of the 17 models for the AECC was the report of the American Accounting Association (AAA) Committee on the Future Structure, Content, and Scope of Accounting Education (the Bedford Committee), appointed in 1984 by AAA President Doyle Williams. The Committee issued its report (AAA 1986) more than three years before the appointment of the AECC. Four committees dealing with implementation issues followed the Bedford Committee report.

AAA President Ray Sommerfeld appointed three of the committees. The Massoud Committee (1986–87) was charged with learning the extent of agreement with the Bedford Committee report. The Smith Committee (1986–87) was to document "the most significant changes in accounting education that have occurred during the past 25 years so that we might better anticipate the near-term difficulties inherent in implementing the [Bedford Committee report]." A parallel committee, chaired by Joe Schultz (1986–87), looked at "how the professorial environment of the accounting professor has changed during the past 25 years so that we might better anticipate the significance of these factors on the near-term implementation issues inherent in the [Bedford Committee report]."

The following year, AAA President Bill Beaver appointed another committee chaired by Joe Schultz (1987–88) to "revisit the [Bedford Committee] report; combine the findings and recommendations of the three committees established by Sommerfeld; and make recommendations regarding implementation."

An AAA publication, *Reorienting Accounting Education: Report on the Environment, Professoriate, and Curriculum of Accounting* (Schultz 1989), included all four committee reports. Despite the significant efforts of these committees, implementation was proceeding slowly. But the pieces were in place. The stage was set. All that was needed was a catalyst.

The Accounting Education Change Commission was appointed in August 1989, and it became the needed catalyst. The appointment of the AECC and the subsequent changes both could have been the result of the same inexorable forces. It may have just taken this long for the recommendations of the Bedford Committee and its follow-up committees to begin to have an influence. If so, the changes in accounting education might have occurred even in the absence of the AECC. Alternatively, the AECC may have been one of the major driving forces behind the changes; without the AECC, we might not be experiencing the curricular changes currently being implemented by nearly every accounting program.

Reality is probably between these two extremes. The AECC has been influential, but it is by no means the only force behind change. Change would have probably happened without the AECC, but it is likely that it would have come more slowly and would have been applied less broadly in the early years.

The purpose of this monograph is to review the seven-year life of the AECC. In the process, I will point out what I consider the successes and failures of the Commission. I will not attempt an empirical evaluation of the impact of the AECC; it is too early to measure whether today's and tomorrow's accounting graduates are better prepared to succeed in professional accounting than were their predecessors. However, I will try to establish the link between changes in accounting programs and the efforts of the Commission. My main theme will be that economic forces made most of the changes in accounting education inevitable. Still, the AECC played two major roles in the process of change. First, it stimulated widespread discussions of changes before they would have naturally arisen. Second, it provided models of change—some more successful than others—that could act as prototypes for other accounting programs wishing to change but not having the resources to develop entirely new approaches. In other words, the AECC was an effective catalyst for change, but only because most of the elements of change were in place when it was formed. Change would have happened without the Commission, but it would not have happened as quickly or as broadly.

When I was Executive Director of the Commission, I was often asked how we would judge whether the Commission was successful. The Commission itself had a task force charged with developing measures of the Commission's success. However, I think there is one overriding measure of success: *that another similar commission is not needed.* The Commission was created for a limited life, initially five years but later extended to seven. In an environment dedicated to continuous improvement, an AECC would not be necessary. It was needed in 1989 because the principles of continuous improvement were not being followed by many in the accounting academy. Those who created the Commission did not foresee a continuing need for it once the inertia was broken. Only if accounting programs retreated again to the complacency of the 1980s, abandoning the process of continuous improvement put in motion by the Commission and other forces of the 1990s, would such intervention in the process be necessary. In other words, the AECC was not charged simply with helping create a one-time change in accounting education. It was charged with instilling in the accounting academy a process of change, one that monitors the capabilities needed by graduates and continually changes (improves) the educational process to achieve those capabilities.

This will not be an objective history of the AECC. I am not a historian, and I have been too close to the Commission to pretend to have an objective view. I believe the AECC had a significant influence on changes in accounting education, primarily in accelerating the change and providing a consistent direction for the changes, but it was not equally successful in all its endeavors. I will try to assess the relative success of various initiatives and examine why each succeeded to the extent it did. I will also examine the internal functioning of the Commission, especially trying to identify the factors that led to whatever success the Commission accomplished.

The AECC has not been without its critics. In fact, many early critics had a significant influence on the Commission. I know my views and actions as a Commission member were altered by several well-reasoned criticisms. On the other hand, some criticisms showed a lack of complete understanding of the environment in which the Commission was operating. I will try to be fair to all of these criticisms in this monograph, but I apologize ahead of time if my involvement on the Commission makes me too defensive with regard to some of them.

I am grateful to the many persons who have given me the opportunity to prepare this monograph and who have helped in its development. First is Gerhard Mueller, the second Chair of the AECC. Gerry had planned to write this monograph until his appointment to the FASB intervened. When he asked me to do it, I was pleased to accept the challenge. Second is Doyle Williams, the first Chair of the Commission. I learned a great deal from Doyle, and my debt to him will be obvious to those who read the monograph. Third is all of the Commission members. Without their dedication and countless hours devoted to the Commission, it would not have had a great enough impact to warrant this monograph. Finally, the American Accounting Association, especially Executive Directors Paul Gerhardt and Craig Polhemus, provided great support. The AAA Educational Advisory Committee oversaw this monograph's writing and publication. The Committee tried their best to keep me on schedule and to help keep the monograph on target. It provided four reviewers who supplied many helpful comments and corrections. Their efforts have greatly improved the monograph. However, I take ultimate responsibility for the contents, especially the shortcomings.

Chapter 1
THE CLIMATE FOR CHANGE

Background in the Profession and the Academy

American universities have provided education for prospective accountants for most of the twentieth century. There was a great deal of evolutionary change throughout the century, with most of the early changes led by academics who developed innovative textbooks or new academic programs. Often these same academicians were also practicing accountants, and the needs of practice were closely aligned with the educational programs. Graduates obtained jobs in the accounting profession—defined to include public accounting, industry, and government accounting positions—and everyone seemed content.

Until the last third of this century it was difficult to distinguish between the accounting academy and the accounting profession. Prior to the 1960s, accounting academics taught what was practiced in the profession, which was facilitated by the fact that many of the leading accounting faculty were simultaneously practicing accountants. Accounting practitioners were among the leading thinkers and writers, encouraging both practice and academe to change with the times. Conflicts between academic accountants and practitioners were few.

All this changed in the late 1950s and early 1960s. Two major studies challenged business schools and, by implication, accounting departments to become more scholarly.[1] Meanwhile, the accounting profession was becoming more competitive. Both academics and professionals turned within themselves. Academics focused on developing prestige on campus; their constituency became fellow faculty members rather than accounting professionals. Professionals struggled to keep their competitive advantage; there was less time devoted to advancing the profession of accounting and more to developing proprietary methods and techniques to differentiate a firm from its competitors.

The initial impact of the growing separation of the accounting academy and the accounting profession was generally positive. Accounting programs started attracting better students and more resources. Accounting faculty became better trained, especially for research, and a larger percentage of them committed themselves full-time to their academic pursuits. In accounting practice, public accounting firms developed new, innovative services and generally had a thriving business throughout the 1970s. Accountants in industry and government were moving through their organizations into increasingly responsible positions. Surveys showed that accounting education and experience were highly valued by many types of organizations.

However, it didn't take long for problems to develop. By the mid-1980s both academic and professional accountants were struggling. Changes in the regulatory environment, rising expectations as witnessed by growing litigation against accountants, the expanding scope and complexity of accounting services, and exponential advances in information technology were revolutionizing (and threatening) traditional accounting practices. Accountants in most organizations, whether

---

[1] These studies, by the Ford Foundation (Gordon and Howell 1959) and Carnegie Foundation (Pierson 1959), were to significantly change all of business education, thereby also affecting accounting education.

public accounting, industry, or government, had to adapt quickly to changing circumstances. Such adaptation is always difficult, and some leading accounting practitioners felt that accounting educational programs had been especially weak in preparing members of the profession for the changes.

Meanwhile, accounting educators were trying to accommodate an information explosion. The number of rules, regulations, and techniques were expanding more rapidly than the time available to learn them. Until recently it was possible for accounting students to learn the rules and procedures of accounting together with a conceptual understanding of accounting in a four-year undergraduate program. But by the 1980s the learning (memorizing?) of rules and procedures was crowding out the conceptual content of the curriculum. Without a good conceptual base, graduates were not well prepared to adapt to changes.

I believe the concluding sentence of each of the two preceding paragraphs explains why academics and practitioners came together in the late 1980s to call for changes in accounting education. The rhetoric on both sides included many other issues, but the overriding, uniting factor was the need to produce accounting graduates who could adapt to change. Rules, regulations, and techniques have a short half-life, and it is getting shorter as the pace of change accelerates. The challenge to accounting educators is to maintain the technical accounting competence demanded in graduates, while increasing their understanding of accounting and business so that they can adapt and apply their technical skills to new environments.

Frameworks for Accounting Education

As academic and professional accountants started down different paths in the 1960s, at least two different organizations recognized the need to formalize the expectations for accounting graduates. In 1968 the American Accounting Association (AAA), representing academics, staked its claim to leadership in educational policy with the publication of a committee report, "A Restatement of Matters Relating to Educational Policy" (AAA 1968). The preceding year the American Institute of Certified Public Accountants (AICPA), representing practitioners, published a report by Roy and McNeill (1967), *The Common Body of Knowledge for Certified Public Accountants: Horizons for a Profession*, and the following year it published the Beamer Committee report, *Report of the Committee on Education and Education Requirements for CPAs* (AICPA 1969). By the 1980s, these were followed by similar reports from the American Assembly of Collegiate Schools of Business (Porter and McKibbin 1988), Association of Government Accountants (Fox 1981), Federation of Schools of Accountancy (FSA 1982), Institute of Internal Auditors (Barrett et al. 1985), and the National Association of Accountants (now Institute of Management Accountants) (NAA 1986, 1988), in addition to more AAA and AICPA reports. Needles and Powers (1990) indicate that there were 17 different educational programs put forward by these various groups.

Underlying all these reports was the recognition that, with the expansion of accounting knowledge, there was no longer time in a traditional undergraduate accounting education to learn the complete body of knowledge of accounting. Two potential solutions emerged: (1) extend accounting programs to five years of post-secondary education or (2) refocus the curriculum. Many of the studies advocated some combination of each.

First to emerge was the push for requiring a graduate degree for entry to the accounting profession; this has resulted in the regulatory efforts to require five years of education to sit for the Certified Public Accountant (CPA) examination. The premise of this approach was that if there is more to learn, students should spend more time learning it. Some advocates of five-year accounting programs thought the extra time should be spent learning accounting rules, regulations, and techniques in more depth; others thought the time should be spent developing the breadth that had often been sacrificed in an attempt to squeeze more accounting into the curriculum.

This divergence of goals for the added year of education led to regulations in many states that mandated 150 semester-hours of post-secondary education, but were silent on what subjects should be included in the extra coursework and whether this constituted a graduate degree.

Refocusing the curriculum required identifying the most important topics from among the many potential subjects that could be taught in an accounting curriculum. Studies focusing on a "common body of knowledge" traditionally separated knowledge that is crucial to an accounting career from knowledge that may be helpful but is not essential. Entrants to the profession could be held responsible for the common body, and additional knowledge and skills could be developed as needed.

Changing Focus in the 1980s

In the 1980s, the consensus on the common body of knowledge began to erode. Accountants began to realize that no matter how many courses students took, they were not going to be able to know the complete body of accounting rules, regulations, and techniques. A new approach to accounting education was needed.

Many professional schools faced similar situations. For example, pharmacy schools recently started down the path of five-year programs, but soon realized that simply expanding the time in school would not be a long-run solution. They needed to make fundamental changes in the curriculum. Maybe more pertinent to accounting is what happened nearly a century ago in law schools. At that time, it became evident that aspiring lawyers could no longer learn the complete body of the law—it was just too extensive. Instead, law schools, especially the best ones, increasingly focused on teaching students how to think about the law. They taught a process, not a body of knowledge. The process was founded in a conceptual understanding of the law, together with the ability to structure approaches to issues and locate and understand the relevant body of knowledge when needed.

As it became clear to more and more accounting faculty that changes were necessary, three issues remained paramount: (1) what curricular changes should be made (i.e., what should be included in and excluded from the required accounting curriculum and how should it be taught), (2) how should such changes be made, and (3) how will employers of accounting graduates react to the changes.

By the late 1980s there were signs of evolutionary change. But changes in universities usually occur slowly. Changes initiated and driven by faculty were not fast enough for a group representing the major public accounting firms in the U.S. As major customers of accounting programs—that is, employers of accounting graduates—the leaders of the firms became concerned that they would not be competitive in this dawning information age if their main source of talent, university accounting programs, did not change quickly. Rather than sit back and allow academics to debate whether to change, what to change, and how to change, the accounting firms took the initiative. One major result of this initiative was the formation of the Accounting Education Change Commission (AECC) in 1989.

Chapter 2
FORMATION OF THE COMMISSION

In April 1989 the then Big 8 public accounting firms issued what became known as "The Big 8 White Paper" (*Perspectives* 1989).[2] It was signed by the following leaders of the Big 8:

Duane R. Kullberg, Arthur Andersen & Co.

Ray J. Groves, Ernst & Whinney

William L. Gladstone, Arthur Young

Larry D. Horner, Peat Marwick Main & Co.

Peter R. Scanlon, Coopers & Lybrand

Shaun F. O'Malley, Price Waterhouse

J. Michael Cook, Deloitte Haskins & Sells

Edward A. Kangas, Touche Ross

The White Paper detailed the firms' expectations of accounting graduates. It also suggested the formation of the Accounting Education Change Commission and promised funding for the Commission. Understanding the motivation for the White Paper helps to understand the need for the AECC.

Sponsors' Task Force

In 1988 the managing partners of the Big 8 firms agreed that many graduates of existing accounting programs lacked the skills and abilities to succeed in the competitive environment of the 1990s and the twenty-first century. Each appointed an expert within his firm to a combined task force to explore solutions to this problem. This group, later to become known as the Sponsors' Education Task Force (hereafter the Sponsors' Task Force), prepared the above-mentioned White Paper titled *Perspectives on Education: Capabilities for Success in the Accounting Profession*, which is included as appendix B of this monograph. The White Paper outlined the "partnership of faculty and practitioners" necessary to achieve the desired enhancements to accounting education.

The White Paper had two purposes. First, it specified skills and knowledge needed to succeed in the accounting profession. A significant inclusion was the emphasis on skills, specifically communication skills, intellectual skills, and interpersonal skills. In addition, the required knowledge base included general knowledge and organizational and business knowledge, as well as accounting and auditing knowledge. Finally, the White Paper maintained that the accounting and auditing education should not be directed simply at passing the CPA examination. Instead, "the focus should be on developing analytical and conceptual thinking—versus memorizing rapidly expanding professional standards."

The second purpose was to present a program to accomplish the changes necessary for accounting graduates to enter the profession with the requisite skills and knowledge. Recognizing

---

[2] The White Paper was widely distributed, as described in a cover letter accompanying it: "Because of the importance of the issues discussed in this paper, we are distributing copies to a number of parties concerned with education for accounting. Within academia, we will be forwarding this paper to college and university presidents, deans of business schools, chairmen of accounting departments and accounting faculty. Copies also will be sent to state boards of accountancy, state societies of CPAs and officers of the American Accounting Association, American Institute of Certified Public Accountants, American Assembly of Collegiate Schools of Business, National Association of State Boards of Accountancy, Financial Executives Institute and National Association of Accountants. All United States senators and representatives will receive copies, as will officials of interested government agencies."

that changes in accounting programs and curricula are the purview of faculty, the authors of the White Paper recommended that the American Accounting Association (AAA) "take the leadership role" in implementing the change process. In essence, they proposed using Big 8 resources and AAA ideas to address an issue that was important to both parties.

American Accounting Association Involvement

The recommendations might have ended there, with the profession sitting back and waiting for the accounting academy to embrace and implement the needed changes. However, many practitioners (including a majority of the Sponsors' Task Force) believed that the AAA had neither the structure nor the resources to successfully undertake such a task on its own. The AAA, through its dedicated voluntary leadership and committee structure, had a reputation for high intellectual content in its committee reports and actions. But it did not have a successful track record in moving quickly, and there was little evidence that its reports had much direct impact on accounting programs. For example, the Bedford Committee report had been issued three years previously, and four follow-up committees had issued reports, yet few of the reports' recommendations had found their way into any actual curricula.

Therefore, two specific proposals were put forth in the White Paper:

1) A "coordinating committee" should be set up to guide the educational change process. All significant stakeholders should be included, including but not limited to "the AICPA, AAA, AACSB, National Association of State Boards of Accountancy (NASBA), Financial Executives Institute (FEI), National Association of Accountants (NAA) [now the Institute of Management Accountants (IMA)] and the major firms."

2) The Big 8 should provide "leadership, guidance, and financial resources" to the coordinating committee. To this end, the firms made a "five-year commitment of up to $4 million to support the development of stimulating and relevant curricula."

In early 1989, Sponsors' Task Force members approached AAA President Gerhard G. Mueller and President-Elect John Simmons to explore and encourage the AAA's endorsement of this plan. At its April 1989 meeting, the AAA Executive Committee authorized the President and President-Elect to organize the Accounting Education Change Commission (AECC). The AAA noted the approval as follows:

> At its meeting in April 1989, the AAA Executive Committee authorized the President and President-Elect jointly to establish an Accounting Education Change Commission. The Accounting Education Change Commission would structure the needed processes: to address the educational changes; to award grants and contracts to individuals, organizations and institutions as appropriate; to carry out as-needed experimentation and preparation of alternate educational processes; and to carry out conferences and workshops as needed to accomplish changes in accounting education consistent with the Bedford Report, its follow-up reports and the objectives noted in the *Perspectives on Education Capabilities* Report. In the summer of 1989, the AAA signed a Memorandum of Understanding with accounting firms that led to the establishment of the AECC. (AAA 1995)

Memorandum of Understanding

Professors Mueller and Simmons worked with the Sponsors' Task Force to develop a structure and operating procedures for the AECC. A Memorandum of Understanding between the sponsoring firms and the AAA was signed on June 30, 1989.[3] The Memorandum specified the following objective of the AECC:

---

[3] Signing the Memorandum were Gerhard G. Mueller and John K. Simmons representing the AAA, Doyle Z. Williams representing the AECC, and Richard Shafer, Francis N. Bonsignore, Donald Dupont, Robert K. Elliott, Robert McDowell, Bruce Mantia, Lester Sussman, and David A. Wilson representing the sponsoring firms.

The overall objective of the Accounting Education Change Commission is to foster changes in the academic preparation of accountants consistent with the goal of improving their capabilities for successful professional careers in practice. These capabilities are described in the sponsoring firms' White Paper, *Perspectives on Education: Capabilities for Success in the Accounting Profession*, and in the American Accounting Association report of the Committee on the Future Structure, Content and Scope of Accounting Education (Bedford Committee report). Providing such capabilities will require both curriculum reengineering and supportive institutional changes by educational, professional, licensing, and accreditation bodies, *inter alia*, all with the ultimate goal of serving the public interest through the improved education of accountants. The Accounting Education Change Commission has been formed to pursue the realization of these objectives.

In the Memorandum, the sponsoring firms also conditionally pledged $4 million to fund the AECC, with the funding channeled through the American Accounting Association. The conditions for the grant were that the provisions of the Memorandum be carried out.

The Memorandum established the AAA as the parent body of the AECC. The AAA was to create and charge the Commission, appoint, reappoint, remove, or replace Commission members, approve AECC operating procedures, and provide appropriate fiscal oversight. Especially important was the AAA's responsibility to terminate the Commission when either (1) it failed to make acceptable progress or (2) it completed its work. The Commission's task was clearly seen as temporary, its life limited. It was not intended to be the type of permanent organization, along the lines of the National Science Foundation, that Previts (1991) advocated as necessary for continued timely improvements in accounting education.

The AAA President and President-Elect jointly appointed AECC members to two-year renewable terms. No approval of either the AAA Executive Committee or the Sponsors' Task Force was required, although in practice their advice was generally sought. The Memorandum specifically addressed eight positions on the Commission. The two leadership positions, Chairman and Executive Director will be discussed later. Six additional members represented specific constituencies. The Memorandum stated that each of the following organizations would be asked to nominate three to five individuals from which the AAA President and President-Elect would select the AECC representatives: Sponsors' Task Force, American Assembly of Collegiate Schools of Business, American Institute of Certified Public Accountants, Financial Executives Institute, National Association of Accountants, and National Association of State Boards of Accountancy. This requirement assured that a broad cross-section of professional accounting would be represented.

The total size of the Commission was not established in the Memorandum. It simply stated that the "AAA shall also appoint a sufficient number of accounting faculty and nonaccountants to assure the Commission of the necessary depth and breadth of input." Professors Mueller and Simmons appointed eight such persons (five accounting professors, one accounting practitioner, one university president, and one education expert), bringing the total AECC membership to 16.

In addition to the regular members, there were two ex-officio members who had full participation rights but no vote: (1) the AAA's Director of Education and (2) the AICPA's Vice President, Education. The Memorandum of Understanding called these two "invited guests," but they were treated the same as other Commission members except for the voting privilege.

Initial Commission Membership

Extensive recruiting efforts by Professors Mueller and Simmons produced a Commission that clearly met the criterion in the Memorandum of Understanding that members be "committed and highly respected individuals who can influence both the Commission and the other organizations with which they are affiliated." For its first two years of operation, the Commission consisted of the following 18 members (including affiliations for those nominated by a specific constituency):

Steven R. Berlin (FEI)
John F. Chironna (NAA [IMA])
Robert K. Elliott (Sponsors' Task Force)
Nathan T. Garrett (NASBA)
Charles T. Horngren
Donald E. Kieso
Paul L. Locatelli, S. J.
James K. Loebbecke
Melvin C. O'Connor
Vincent M. O'Reilly

Ray M. Sommerfeld
Joan S. Stark
A. Marvin Strait (AICPA)
Gary L. Sundem, Executive Director
Richard R. West (AACSB)
Doyle Z. Williams, Chairman

Ex Officio:
Rick Elam (AICPA)
Corine T. Norgaard (AAA)

AECC Chairman

The success of an organization such as the AECC depends heavily on its leadership. The AECC was fortunate to have Doyle Z. Williams as its first Chairman. The position of Chairperson was a part-time position with a three-year renewable term. Williams was in the position for four-and-a-half years, before being followed by Gerhard G. Mueller for the last two-and-a-half years of the Commission's life.

Both Williams and Mueller were acknowledged by fellow Commission members as effective leaders. However, because Williams was the initial Chairman and presided for more than half the life of the Commission, his impact was especially apparent. As the AAA president who appointed the Bedford Committee and a strong supporter of both professional schools of accountancy and 150-semester-hour accounting programs, Williams already had a reputation as an accounting reformer. However, to his credit, his agenda did not become the Commission's agenda. Instead, he created an open atmosphere where the initial 18 members formulated the Commission's agenda and approach. Chapter 3, "Setting the Direction," will describe the process.

Two characteristics of Doyle Williams's leadership were especially important in the early days of the AECC. First, he was output oriented, and second, he could achieve consensus within a diverse group. The Commission moved quickly under Williams, meeting the mandate of the Sponsors' Task Force but generating criticisms of moving too fast (see, for example, Barefield 1991).

The Commission was established to take actions, not prepare reports. Its success would be measured by real change in accounting education, not by the eloquence of its pronouncements. Williams pushed the Commission to tackle issues where a real impact could be made. Further, he wanted initial actions to begin immediately, not only after prolonged discussion. The strategy was to identify the "low-hanging fruit" and pick it quickly, even before a plan had been devised for picking the harder-to-reach fruit. I believe this strategy was one of the main reasons that the AECC had a large impact almost immediately within the accounting academy. It also accounted for some of the controversies along the way.

For the AECC to move quickly, it was necessary for the Commission to achieve consensus on its objectives and the initial steps for accomplishing them. Many members of the original Commission have commented on the skill with which Doyle Williams accomplished this. Under his leadership, a diverse set of individuals committed the time and effort necessary to work out differences and subjugate their personal agendas to the good of the Commission. Mel O'Connor praised Williams's leadership style by saying, "Doyle had a way of getting you to commit huge blocks of time and energy to further the goals of the Commission and at the same time think that he was doing you a favor" (O'Connor 1996).

The goal of those establishing the AECC was to select a strong, dynamic, respected leader. They got that in Doyle Williams. However, because of his well-known and outspoken positions on many issues of accounting education, sometimes outsiders read things into the AECC's agenda that were not there. I believe that was a small price to pay for the outstanding leadership that Williams provided in the Commission's early years.

Because I was not involved with the Commission during Gerry Mueller's term as Chairman, I know less about his impact. In a sense, Gerry's influence was felt throughout the life of the Commission because, as AAA President, he (together with John Simmons) signed the Memorandum of Understanding and appointed the initial Commission members. He then stepped aside until he was appointed to the Commission in August 1992 and took over as Chairman in January 1994. He had the unenviable task of maintaining the Commission's momentum while phasing out its operation. Although creating the Commission's agenda and formulating a strategy to accomplish it was more exciting, the implementation phase under Mueller's leadership was essential to the success of the Commission. From all accounts, and from the successes in grant project completion, dissemination of grant project results, and hand-off of operations to the AAA, the Commission continued to flourish under Gerry Mueller's leadership.

Executive Director

The Memorandum of Understanding specified a second leadership position for the AECC, an Executive Director. Two characteristics of this position were especially influential in how the Commission operated: (1) the position was a full-time paid position to provide staffing support for the Commission, and (2) the Executive Director was a full member of the Commission. The first provided a person with the time and incentive to devote full attention to the Commission; the second allowed that person to speak with the full authority of the Commission.

The importance of the position of Executive Director cannot be dismissed. (As the first Executive Director, I could be biased, but others have expressed similar views.) Without an Executive Director with the two characteristics in the preceding paragraph, the Commission would not have had as large an impact, or at least its impact would have been slower in coming. A pure staff person could have handled the administrative functions of the position, but would not have had the needed credibility in representing the Commission. An academic on a part-time appointment would have had less time and more distractions, preventing him or her from complete immersion in Commission activities.

With the appointment of Gary Sundem as the first Executive Director, the organizers found someone who was a good complement to Doyle Williams. As a Stanford Ph.D. and a former editor of *The Accounting Review*, Sundem came from a strong research tradition. Although the Commission focused on the teaching role of faculty and accounting programs, it was important to also recognize the role of research in maintaining the vitality of the profession and its educational programs. When the Commission was accused of "research-bashing" (Barefield 1991), Sundem and his academic colleagues on the Commission maintained that there is a synergy between research (or, more generally, scholarly activities) and teaching. It is the *over-emphasis* on either one of these that leads to problems, and the late 1980s seemed to be a time of over-emphasis on research. It was the task of the research-oriented members of the Commission to make sure the pendulum did not swing too far the opposite way. It was also a time of legitimate criticisms of the nature of much accounting research (see Beaver [1992, 137–139] for an excellent discussion of this point), and it was important that these criticisms not be generalized to all accounting research.

Sundem also brought a management-accounting perspective to the Commission. Whereas Williams was active in the California Society of CPAs and the AICPA, Sundem had been involved in the Institute of Management Accountants (as Seattle Chapter President and a member of the National Board of Directors) and the Financial Executives Institute. He had little previous connection with the Big 8, so he could more easily answer the critics who thought the Commission was biased in favor of preparation for public accounting careers, especially for careers in the large firms.

Sundem was Executive Director only two years, but he continued to champion the AECC agenda the following two years as President-Elect and then President of the AAA. In 1991, Doyle Williams was asked to add the Executive Director duties to his Chairmanship when Sundem was elected AAA President-Elect. At the same time a position of Vice-Chairman was created and filled by William Shenkir. It was an unpaid position with responsibility for representing the Commission but with no specific administrative duties. When Doyle Williams assumed the position of Dean of the College of Business Administration at the University of Arkansas in 1993, he relinquished the position of AECC Executive Director and at the end of the year also relinquished the Chairmanship. On July 1, 1993, Richard E. Flaherty was appointed Executive Director and held the position for the last three years of the Commission's life.

Flaherty was especially successful in leading the effort to disseminate the results from the grant projects. He was well known in the academic accounting community, and he spent a great deal of time making presentations around the country about how to go about changing accounting programs.

Turnover of Membership

The original Commission members remained in place for two years. Much of the success of the Commission was due to the espirit des corps among these 18 individuals. They shared the excitement of creation and formed a strong bond of common goals. However, the Memorandum of Understanding clearly anticipated rotation of membership. The Chairman had an initial three-year term, the Executive Director had an initial one-year term, and all Commissioners had two-year terms. All were renewable annually thereafter.

Thus, at the end of the second year, membership changes were made. Gary Sundem resigned because of potential conflicts of interest with his AAA duties, and Nathan Garrett and Richard West also stepped down. They were replaced by Sarah Blake, Katherine Schipper, and William Shenkir, who was appointed Vice Chairman. In addition, Robert Ingram replaced Corrine Norgaard as the AAA Director of Education and thus took her place on the Commission. The quality of these replacements assured that the momentum of the Commission would not wane. The pace of four meetings per year continued through the 1992–93 academic year as emphasis switched from setting the direction to monitoring change activities and providing tools to help schools change their accounting programs.

Another five of the original Commission members completed their service at the end of 1991–92: Steve Berlin, Charles Horngren, James Loebbecke, Vincent O'Reilly, and Ray Sommerfeld. They were replaced by Penny Flugger, David Landsittel, Gerhard Mueller, Peter Wilson, and Robert Witt. It was clear that Commission membership was attractive enough to continue attracting top-level members.

The 1993–94 year marked the first year that a majority of the Commission members had not been on the initial Commission. At the beginning of that year John Chironna, Donald Kieso, and Marvin Strait were replaced by Richard Flaherty, James Naus, and Stanley Pylipow, and Jan Williams replaced Robert Ingram as the AAA representative. In addition, on January 1, 1994 Barron Harvey replaced Doyle Williams, and Gerhard Mueller took over the Commission Chairmanship.

The end of the 1993–94 year marked the departure of two original Commission members who were especially influential on the direction of the Commission: Joan Stark and Robert Elliott. Their replacements were Eugene Rice and David Pearson. By this time only two original members, Mel O'Connor and Paul Locatelli, and one ex-officio member, Rick Elam, remained. During 1995 Rick Elam left the AICPA, thus vacating his ex-officio seat, and Mike Diamond replaced Jan Williams as the AAA representative. That marked the end of changes in Commission membership. Mel O'Connor and Paul Locatelli were the only members who saw the Commission through from start to finish.

Chapter 3
SETTING THE DIRECTION

The Accounting Education Change Commission brought together 18 individuals, all committed to change in accounting education along the lines of the Big 8 White Paper and the Bedford Committee report. But they differed in perspective, background, and experience. While there may have been a natural agreement on general goals, there was no reason to expect agreement on specific objectives or strategies to achieve them. To achieve the quick impact desired by the sponsors, a plan was needed quickly. Three meetings were scheduled within a 15-week period to develop this plan.

Initial AECC Meetings

The first meeting of the AECC was held September 8, 1989, in Chicago.[4] The focus of this meeting and the following two meetings (October 31–November 1 in Atlanta and December 14–15 in San Francisco) was to agree on a direction for change and a mechanism for achieving the needed changes.

The 18 Commissioners represented a wide range of academic and professional interests, and all had ideas about how accounting education should change. Their appointment to the Commission indicated a commitment to change, but it quickly became clear that all change agendas were not alike. A combination of outside presentations and internal discussions put the various alternatives on the table. Vigorous debate brought out the common factors and the areas of disagreement.

Due in large part to the skillful leadership of Chairman Doyle Williams, the Commission expeditiously coalesced around a common set of basic objectives. Once the Commission reached agreement, personal agendas took a back seat to the Commission's agenda. I believe that a major factor in the Commission's success was the willingness and ability of all 18 members to buy into the Commission's agenda. Throughout the life of the Commission there were discussions and disagreements during Commission meetings, but once issues were decided, Commission members went forth with a united front.

Two early decisions were instrumental in setting the directions the Commission would take. First, it committed itself to concern for all career paths in accounting. Second, it avoided the politically charged debate on the need for five years of postsecondary education for professional accountants.

The first official action of the AECC was approval of a resolution committing the Commission to be concerned with accounting careers broadly defined:

The Commission will address the preparation of accountants for careers in public accounting as practiced in large, medium, and small firms, corporate accounting (including financial management, controllership, treasury, financial analysis, planning and budgeting, cost accounting, internal audit, systems, tax, and general accounting), and governmental and non-profit accounting....When the Commission uses terms such as "accounting careers," "accounting profession," or "accounting

---

[4] The Commission meetings were rotated to different cities in different parts of the country to allow interested persons to observe a meeting in person without undue travel time and costs.

professionals," these terms are understood to refer to accounting broadly defined, including all career paths listed...above. (AECC 1989b, 3)

The Commission made a concerted effort to avoid the stigma of catering only to preparation for public accounting careers.

Sponsorship of the Commission by the major public accounting firms gave some observers the impression that the changes advocated by the Commission would be in the best interest of such firms, possibly to the detriment of other professional accounting careers. For example, a paper by Davis and Sherman (1994) "raises questions concerning the apparent lack of independence of the Commission and the potential that the AECC may have indeed been 'captured' by the accounting firms which have financed its operation." The paper "further questions whether the interests of all stakeholders have been adequately represented in the Commission's initiatives." However, both industry and small/medium public accounting firms were represented on the Commission. (A legitimate criticism is that government and nonprofit accountants were not represented.) I believe the vast majority of the AECC members were sensitive to the needs of various professional accounting careers. Further, subsequent studies by the Institute of Management Accountants and the Financial Executives Institute have called for most of the same changes as the AECC advocated (see Siegel and Sorensen 1994; Larsen and Ahlstrand 1991).

A less formal, but equally important, decision was to focus on the learning experience provided for the students rather than the administrative structure of accounting programs. Specifically, the Commission elected to not enter the debate over whether college and university accounting programs should be four or five years in length. This was a politically charged issue for which there was a diversity of opinion on the Commission and no obviously right answer. Instead of entering this debate, the Commission supported diversity in the way accounting programs are packaged. However, regardless of the length of the program or the titles and lengths of courses, a common set of learning objectives emerged. The Commission did not develop (or even seriously discuss) a "model curriculum"; degrees and course titles were secondary to the subject matter and process of education. The focus was on students' learning objectives and how best to achieve them.

By diffusing one potential criticism and avoiding another, the AECC tried to pave the way to internal consensus and public acceptance. This worked for internal consensus, but unfortunately, public acceptance did not come as easily. Because the campaign to require five years of accounting education was driven by those in public accounting (and the AICPA, in particular), and because many of those advocating the changes sought by the AECC were also advocates of the five-year requirement, the issues became muddled in many minds. This was exacerbated by the fact that AECC Chairman Williams was an outspoken advocate of five-year programs, despite the fact that he carefully avoided support of five-year programs when speaking on behalf of the Commission. As a result, those opposed to mandated five-year programs in accounting and those advocating less of a public-accounting focus in accounting programs were less inclined to support AECC recommendations. Why? Because they thought AECC reforms were a foot in the door for a public-accounting-driven move to five-year programs.

Representation on the Commission

Even before its first meeting, the AECC was criticized for ignoring important stakeholders. Although the Commission included a broad range of stakeholders, it was not possible to include every interest group. One major group left off the Commission was government and nonprofit accountants. Fortunately, several such accountants provided input to the Commission so that their views could be recognized.

The Commission seemed to be more concerned about the under-representation of minorities, probably because minorities are more likely to be affected differently than are others by changes in accounting education. Between the Commission's first and second meetings, Executive Director

Sundem visited Howard University, St. Augustine's College, and the Seattle chapter of the National Association of Black Accountants. He reported that members of those organizations generally supported the thrust of the changes sought by the Commission, but they wanted specific consideration of their impact on minority students. The Commission decided that the best way to achieve this was not with a special "minority" committee or task force but by including minorities on many of the Commission's task forces.

Informing the Commission

Early in the life of the Commission it became clear that many individuals had much knowledge to offer the Commission. Therefore, throughout the life of the Commission, the members were continually being updated on topics that affected their activities. A large number of individuals briefed the Commission on various topics. Of course, many Commission members shared their expertise where appropriate, representatives of the grant schools made presentations about progress, and AAA presidents and other officers often met with the Commission. In addition, the following persons made presentations to the Commission during the years noted:

- B. Needles and M. Powers—"A Comparative Study of the Common Body of Knowledge for Accountants," 1989
- M. Diamond and K. Pincus—Curriculum changes at the University of Southern California, 1989
- R. Laing and M. Larsen—Financial Executives Research Foundation survey on the opinions and attitudes of financial executives on the education required for success as a financial executive, 1990
- D. Skadden—Most recent thoughts of the AACSB Task Force on Accreditation, 1990
- H. Lasker and A. Cantrell—A study that Applied Learning Spectrum did for KPMG Peat Marwick on the knowledge, skills, and abilities required at various levels in the organization and where such knowledge, skills, and abilities were obtained, 1990
- J. D. Edwards—Report on the activities of the Education Committee of the International Federation of Accountants, 1990
- J. Rubin—Update on the activities of the AACSB Accreditation Task Force, 1990
- A. T. Nelson—Discussion about the requirements for a minimum number of accounting hours included in the implementation guidelines for the AICPA/NASBA Model Accountancy Bill, 1990
- M. Helitzer—Proposal by *New Accountant* to prepare a book on the AECC, 1991
- R. Barefield, W. Bentz, and T. Williams—Feedback on the Commission's activities, 1991
- M. Blood—A summary of AACSB activities involving outcome measurement, 1991
- L. Hale, C. Skousen, and R. Pitt—Proposal from Beta Alpha Psi to fund two video program modules to promote accounting careers, 1991
- J. Blum—Report on the results of the "Practice Analysis of Certified Public Accountants in Public Accounting" commissioned by the AICPA's Board of Examiners, 1991
- T. Powell and R. Paligo—Description of the educational initiatives undertaken by the Institute of Internal Auditors, 1992
- L. Davidson—Comprehensive accounting curriculum development project at Florida International University, 1992
- R. Baechle—An overview of the business ethics program sponsored by Arthur Andersen & Co., 1992
- C. Tierney and V. Robinson—Discussion of the need to include the topics of government accounting and auditing in the accounting curriculum, 1992
- H. Roberts—Applications of Total Quality Management to business education, 1992
- N. Walker—The Price Waterhouse approach to continuing professional education, 1992

- T. Beauchemin—The Enterprise 2000 approach to the change process, 1993
- J. Searfoss—The Deloitte & Touche program on "Enhancing the Learning Experience," 1993
- L. Scott—A program to promote continuous improvement for academic accounting programs sponsored by the Practice Involvement Committee of the Administrators of Accounting Programs Group, 1993
- J. Fernandes and G. Sumners—Institute of Internal Auditors program on "How We are Enhancing the Early Employment Experiences of Internal Auditors," 1993
- C. Clark, K. Pincus, L. Scott, and J. Searfoss—Report from the Federation of Schools of Accountancy Committee on Implementing Change, 1993
- P. Chenok—Expressed AICPA's support for the work of the Commission, 1994
- J. Hunnicutt—Update on recent AICPA developments dealing with accounting education, 1996

Strategic Planning

The unification of the AECC members was aided by a successful strategic-planning effort facilitated by a consultant, Eric R. Baron, of Consultative Resources Corporation. By the end of 1989, the Commission had established a mission statement and five goals. The Mission was similar, but not identical, to the objectives put forth in the *Memorandum of Understanding*:

> The mission of the Accounting Education Change Commission (AECC) is to be a catalyst for improving the academic preparation of accountants, so that entrants to the accounting profession possess the skills, knowledge, and attitudes required for success in accounting career paths. The AECC seeks to enhance the quality of education for accountants consistent with the objectives of the AAA's Bedford Committee Report and the Sponsoring Firms' White Paper, *Perspectives on Education: Capabilities for Success in the Accounting Profession*. (AECC 1990, inside cover)

By February 1990, the Chairman and Executive Director had established 19 task forces, later reduced to 16 by combining task forces with overlapping objectives, to execute the activities needed to accomplish the goals. Each Commission member was appointed to one or more task forces, with specific duties tied directly to the objectives of the task force. In addition, the task forces included non-Commission members whose expertise was especially valuable.

Because the task forces did most of the actual work of the Commission, the following section will list all 16 of them with their membership and charges. There was a subtle but significant evolution in the language used by the Commission in the goal statements. The discussion of "changes" in accounting education now became one of "improvements." Although this change may be obvious in hindsight, it was important to the Commission. As Barefield (1991, 306) stated in an insightful critique of the AECC, "[F]orces for change have come from the AAA, the AICPA, and the national firms...[and] the convergence of their views is more toward agreement on the need for change than it is toward a common focus on what that change should be." Although both the *Memorandum of Understanding* and the AECC Mission Statement accepted the Bedford Committee and the Big 8 White Paper as the authoritative basis for the direction of change, the AECC goals stated a need to make sure that changes advocated by the Commission were actually improvements.

How was the Commission to determine whether changes are improvements? Barefield (1991, 309) pointed out that the White Paper is "too 'green' or untested a foundation on which to build sweeping educational change." It is hard to disagree with the assertion that many of the suggested changes were not yet proven to be improvements. Yet management, unlike scientists, sometimes cannot wait for such proof. I often tell my students that management decision making is "making irrevocable decisions based on inadequate information." We would always like additional information, but sometimes decisions must be made based on a "best guess" as to their consequences. At times, management of educational institutions must do this also. The Commission at least used its collective wisdom to make "best guesses" at what would constitute improvements, but it remains to be seen if they will be proven to be correct. Nevertheless, the AECC did not blindly accept suggested changes as improvements. Instead, it developed its own views of what parts of the Bedford Committee report and Big 8 White Paper to emphasize.

AECC Task Forces

Sixteen AECC task forces were appointed in February 1990. Categorized by the goal they were intended to achieve, the task forces were:

Goal 1: Identify the goals of education for accountants

Task Force 1A: Objectives of Education for Accountants
James K. Loebbecke, AECC, Chair
Gary L. Sundem, AECC

Charge: Prepare an exposure draft of a position statement on "Objectives of Education for Accountants," drawing from the report of the Bedford Committee and the *Perspectives* paper. Continue to monitor the educational and professional environments for implications for accounting education that may necessitate revision of the position statement.

Goal 2: Foster an environment for improvements in the education of accountants

Task Force 2A: Leadership Support
A. Marvin Strait, AECC, Chair
Steven R. Berlin, AECC
John F. Chironna, AECC
Robert Ellyson, Coopers & Lybrand
Thomas F. Keller, Duke University
Richard J. Lewis, Michigan State University
Paul L. Locatelli, AECC
Melvin C. O'Connor, AECC

Charge: (1) Identify leaders in academe and the profession, by virtue of their position and/or their influence, and develop strategies for enlisting their support for changing accounting education. (2) Identify stakeholder organizations and develop strategies for the AECC establishing linkages with them.

Task Force 2B: Information Dissemination
Gary L. Sundem, AECC
Doyle Z. Williams, AECC

Charge: Disseminate information about the need for change; develop a speaking program for the AECC; publish information about the need for change and about activities of the AECC; conduct symposia on implementing change in accounting education.

Task Force 2C: Early Employment Experience
Robert K. Elliott, AECC, Chair
John K. Chironna, AECC
James W. Deitrick, University of Texas at Austin
Brian J. Jemelian, Price Waterhouse
Vincent M. O'Reilly, AECC
A. Marvin Strait, AECC

Charge: Develop a strategy for addressing the effective interfacing of the education of the "new" accountant with the initial (2 to 3 years) employment experience; consideration should also be given to recruiting signaling on campuses and continuing professional education efforts by employers.

Task Force 2D: Regulatory Issues
Nathan T. Garrett, AECC, Chair

Rick Elam, AECC
Ladelle Hyman, Texas Southern University
Harold Langenderfer, University of North Carolina at Chapel Hill
Charge: Develop a strategy to promote desired changes in Federal, State, and other regulations that affect the accounting educational environment, with particular attention given to the joint AICPA/NASBA Model Bill, State legislation, and board rules implementing the 150-hour requirement, and the timing of the CPA Examination.

Goal 3: Promote implementation of improvements in the education of accountants

Task Force 3A: Grant Program
Doyle Z. Williams, AECC, Chair
Gary L. Sundem, AECC, Vice-Chair
Charge: Develop and propose policies and procedures for conducting the grant program to provide an incentive for experimentation in implementing desired changes in accounting education.

Task Force 3B: Faculty Development
Ray M. Sommerfeld, AECC, Chair
Charles T. Horngren, AECC
Corine T. Norgaard, AECC
Jan R. Williams, University of Tennessee
Charge: To recommend to the AECC strategies for (1) developing faculty teaching capabilities, in doctoral programs and in continuing education for current faculty, consistent with the AECC's "Objectives for Education of Accountants"; and (2) developing faculty interest and capabilities for program innovation and experimentation.

Task Force 3C: Student Recruiting
Rick Elam, AECC, Chair
Steven R. Berlin, AECC
Barron Harvey, Howard University
Charge: Develop a strategy for attracting high-quality students to the study of accounting.

Task Force 3D: Two-Year Schools
Corine T. Norgaard, AECC, Chair
Greg Bischoff, Houston Community College
Dennis Greer, Utah Valley Community College
Tom Hilgerman, St. Louis Community College
Lynn Mazzola, Nassau Community College
Gary L. Sundem, AECC
Charge: Develop a strategy for involving community and junior colleges in accounting education change.

Goal 4: Reduce impediments to improvements in the education of accountants

Task Force 4A: Faculty Incentives
Donald E. Kieso, AECC, Chair
Melvin C. O'Connor, AECC
Ronald J. Patten, DePaul University
Richard R. West, AECC
Arthur R. Wyatt, Arthur Andersen & Co.
Charge: To develop and recommend a strategy to the AECC for increasing faculty incentives for undertaking curriculum development, engaging in educational experimentation and research, and developing effective teaching strategies. Consideration should be given to strategies for altering

typical faculty reward systems, issuing a position statement, working with other organizations (e.g., accrediting bodies), and other approaches.

Task Force 4B: University Support
    Vincent M. O'Reilly, AECC, Chair
    John L. Kramer, University of Florida
    Cecil Mackey, Michigan State University
    Ray M. Sommerfeld, AECC
Charge: To develop and recommend to the AECC a strategy for increasing the level of recognition among university and business school administrators of the importance of high-quality accounting education. Special consideration should be given to developing a strategy for positioning the accounting discipline in a more positive light among the major universities.

Task Force 4C: Instructional Materials
    Charles T. Horngren, AECC, Chair
    Barry Cushing, Pennsylvania State University
    Michael A. Diamond, University of Southern California
    Robert K. Elliott, AECC
    Kenneth W. Rethmeier, Harcourt Brace Jovanovich
Charge: Develop a strategy for promoting the preparation and marketing of relevant instructional materials designed to achieve the desired learning outcomes for the education of accountants.

Task Force 4D: Professional Examinations
    Nathan T. Garrett, AECC, Chair
    Rick Elam, AECC
    Michael L. Fetters, Babson College
    Donald E. Kieso, AECC
Charge: Develop a strategy for minimizing the dysfunctional impact of professional examinations on accounting education. Consideration should be given to the timing of such examinations, publication of pass rates as a measure of program quality, and content.

Task Force 4E: Accreditation
    Melvin C. O'Connor, AECC, Chair
    Robert K. Elliott, AECC
    Richard R. West, AECC
Charge: To develop a strategy for influencing accreditation as a positive force for enhancing quality improvements in accounting education and to develop a paper reflecting the AECC's views on accreditation for submission to the AACSB Task Force on Accreditation. Continue to monitor accreditation developments and bring issues to the AECC as warranted.

Goal 5: Measure improvements in the education of accountants

Task Force 5A: Measurement of Educational Change
    James K. Loebbecke, AECC, Chair
    Robert K. Elliott, AECC
    Brent C. Inman, Coopers & Lybrand
    Joan S. Stark, AECC
Charge: To develop and recommend to the AECC a strategy for measuring the results of the Change Commission's efforts to enhance the skills and capabilities of accounting graduates. Consideration should be given to establishing benchmarks and measuring student skills and capabilities over time. Additionally, consideration should be given to measuring changes in faculty responses to the call for educational reform and program changes. Special consideration should be given to measuring change on the campuses of grant recipients.

Task Force 5B: Change Commission Progress
    Vincent M. O'Reilly, AECC, Chair
    Steven R. Berlin, AECC

Charge: To recommend a strategy for measuring the success of the AECC, focusing initially on the Commission's efforts. Consideration should be given to developing an annual report card. In the long term, consideration should be given to the interfacing of these measures with the measurements developed by the Educational Change Task Force.

Revisiting the Strategic Plan

For its first three years the Commission followed the strategic plan and task force organization it originally established. By 1992–93 the environment for change had been significantly altered, and the five-year horizon planned for the Commission was rapidly approaching. Therefore, the Commission revisited its strategic plan.

The original 16 task forces organized around the five goals of the AECC were consolidated into nine task forces and committees in three areas (with the chair shown in parentheses):

- Major thrust task forces:
    * Curriculum Dissemination (Mueller)
    * Faculty Development (Schipper)
    * Assessment (Landsittel)
- Current projects task forces:
    * Early Employment Experience (Elliott)
    * Faculty Incentives (Kieso)
    * Professional Examinations (Blake)
- Chairman coordinated committees:
    * Information Dissemination (Williams)
    * Grant Monitoring (Williams)
    * Strategic Planning (Williams)

Later, two additional sub-groups were established to deal with specific agenda items, an *ad hoc* Articulation Task Force (W. Shenkir, chair) and a Dissemination Conferences Project Team (M. O'Connor, chair).

The main effect of the reorganization was to focus future activities in three areas, curriculum dissemination, faculty development, and assessment. The disposition of the 16 original task forces and my assessment of the success of the disbanded task forces follow:

1A: Objectives of Education for Accountants—Mission accomplished with publication of Position Statement No. One, *Objectives of Education for Accountants*.

2A: Leadership Support—One of the most difficult tasks and one that was only partially successful. Support within the academic accounting community was excellent; within the higher echelons of the practicing accounting community, good but with little penetration into the rank and file; and outside the accounting community, far short of what was hoped. Especially disappointing was lack of recognition and support from deans of business schools, despite many efforts to involve them in the process.

2B: Information Dissemination—A continuing task force that carried out its responsibilities throughout the life of the Commission by publishing articles, making presentations at a large variety of meetings, and conducting symposia.

2C: Early Employment Experience—Continuing task force. Completed task with publication of Issues Statement No. Four, *Improving the Early Employment Experience of Accountants*.

2D: Regulatory Issues—Incorporated into Professional Examinations Task Force, which was ongoing.

3A: Grant Program—Set the criteria, prepared the request for proposals, and recommended proposals to the AECC for funding. After the grant projects were up and running, this task force was replaced by the Curriculum Dissemination Task Force and the Grant Monitoring Committee. The former was one of the major thrusts of the second half of the Commission's life, and the latter was an operational committee making sure the contracts with the grant schools were fulfilled.

3B: Faculty Development—One of the three major thrusts for the second half of the Commission's life. The late Ray Sommerfeld, first chair of this task force, maintained that faculty development was critical to the Commission's success. It became the major continuing activity that the AECC passed on to the American Accounting Association, with the long-term success of the Commission still riding on the AAA's success in this area.

3C: Student Recruiting—Collected and disseminated materials from schools on strategies for student recruiting. Much of this task force's agenda became subsumed under other activities such as the Two-Year Schools Task Force and the grant projects.

3D: Two-Year Schools—Major progress was made with publication of Issues Statement No. 3, *The Importance of Two-Year Colleges for Accounting*, but relationships between two- and four-year schools remains problematic in many areas. Later, an *ad hoc* task force was established to carry forward the issue of articulation between two- and four-year schools, resulting in publication of Issues Statement No. 6, *Transfer of Academic Credit for the First Course in Accounting Between Two-Year and Four-Year Colleges*.

4A: Faculty Incentives—A continuing task force that completed its charge with publication of Issues Statement No. Five, *Evaluating and Rewarding Effective Teaching*. This task force did a good job with a limited part of the broader charge. To significantly affect the faculty performance evaluation and reward system is a monumental task, and the main thing this task force could to was to bring the issue to the table.

4B: University Support—This was another extremely difficult task, and little progress was made. Institutional support at the universities of the grant recipients was good, but little influence on university administrators beyond these schools was accomplished.

4C: Instructional Materials—This task force worked primarily behind the scenes, including supporting AAA efforts to recognize curriculum innovations and encouraging publishers to evolve textbooks along lines consistent with AECC recommendations. I would judge their efforts a qualified success. Much lip service was given to accommodating AECC recommendations in most textbooks, and new textbooks and other teaching materials incorporating the recommendations emerged. The end-of-chapter materials of almost every textbook changed to include more active learning options. Still, the majority of the textbook market remained remarkably resistant to major changes.

4D: Professional Examinations—A continuing task force that mainly worked directly with the AICPA Board of Examiners and NASBA. It commented on and thereby influenced the model accountancy bill prepared jointly by the AICPA and NASBA, produced Issues Statement No. 2, *AECC Urges Decoupling of Academic Studies and Professional Accounting Examination Preparation*, and seems to have had some influence on the format and content of the CPA examination (although the extent of the influence is not yet fully known).

4E: Accreditation—This was one of the most successful task forces. Most of its work was done early in the life of the Commission, but even though it did not continue as a task force after reorganization, its members continued to monitor accreditation activities. Although the Commission made no public pronouncements on accreditation, the task force's work with the AACSB had a great influence on the new, mission-based accreditation standards that were approved in April 1991 (see chapter 7 for details).

5A: Measurement of Educational Change—Continued as one of the three major thrusts, relabeled the Assessment Task Force. It was impossible for the task force to develop a complete

assessment program in the short life of the Commission, but it contributed to this development with the publication *of Assessment for the New Curriculum: A Guide for Professional
Accounting Programs* (Gainen and Locatelli 1995).

5B: Change Commission Progress—Developed a framework to keep the Commission focused on
its objectives. Although few concrete measures of success were developed, the task force
monitored activities and undertook periodic surveys to assess the Commission's impact.

Extending the Commission's Life

At a meeting in November 1992, with the original end of the Commission's life less than two
years away, AAA President Gary Sundem presented to the Sponsors' Task Force a proposal to
extend the life of the Commission by two to three years to allow implementation of the initiatives
currently under way. The proposal asked for an additional $1 million for the AECC and another
$500,000 to underwrite a faculty development effort at the AAA that was deemed necessary to
continue the work of the Commission. Accompanying Sundem to the meeting and supporting the
proposal were AAA Past President Art Wyatt, AAA President-Elect Andy Bailey, and AECC
Chairman Doyle Williams. The discussion showed general pleasure with the work of the AECC
but skepticism about the ability of the AAA to carry forward the activities.

The presentation of the proposal started a protracted dialog about the hand-off of AECC activities
to the AAA. Extending the life of the AECC was not particularly controversial, but the additional
$500,000 to the AAA was. Although no immediate commitment was made to extend the life of the
Commission, it was apparent after the November 1992 meeting that the Commission would have some
time beyond August 1994 to complete its activities. On February 28, 1994, a formal agreement was
signed committing the Big 6 Sponsoring Firms to "an additional $1 million to extend the funding of
the Accounting Education Change Commission for *at most* an additional three years through fiscal
1997." In fact, the Commission was terminated at its meeting on August 13, 1996.

The signing of an agreement on October 31, 1994 facilitated the hand-off to the AAA.[5] It
committed the Sponsoring Firms to providing the $500,000 to the AAA's faculty and program
development project in addition to $1 million for the extension of the AECC's life. This document
specified the following about the AECC:

> The additional $1 million approved in February 1994 will be used to extend the administra-
> tive life of the Commission *up to* an additional three years and directed primarily to three
> program areas:
> * Curriculum Dissemination—To effectively disseminate the innovations that are taking place
>   at the grant schools, a number of workshops need to be held to share these results with many
>   accounting faculty.
> * Assessment —To assess impact of accounting education change on both curricula as well as
>   on the skills and knowledge of graduating students.
> * Faculty Development—To work with the American Accounting Association to develop new
>   teaching skills to implement revised and new accounting curriculum.

The Commission completed the curriculum dissemination task rather successfully by the end of its life.
Two major steps were taken in assessment, publication of a monograph (Gainen and Locatelli 1995)
and sponsorship of an assessment workshop. However, assessment is a complex issue that will require
continuing attention. Finally, although most of the Commission's activities had some faculty development components to them, the main thrust in faculty development was passed to the AAA.

---

[5]   Signing the agreement for the Big 6 Sponsors' Education Task force were: Brent C. Inman, Coopers & Lybrand; Dennis R.
Reigle, Arthur Andersen & Co.; Mark M. Chain, Deloitte & Touche; Charles B. Eldridge, Ernst & Young; Robert K. Elliott,
KPMG Peat Marwick; and Larry P. Scott, Price Waterhouse. All six of these signers also made significant contributions to the
work of the Commission in a variety of ways.

It is too early to fully judge the AAA's faculty development effort, and such an evaluation is beyond the scope of this monograph. However, I think it is off to a good start after some initial rough spots. In 1993, the Sponsor's Task Force authorized use of part of the $500,000 requested by the AAA to undertake a needs analysis in faculty development. The commitment of the full amount would be contingent on the results of the analysis. In 1994, the AAA hired Strategic Initiatives, Inc., to undertake a needs analysis in faculty development. Although the study was highly criticized by some because it came up with few new insights, it served the purpose of confirming the importance of faculty development and the approach advocated by the Commission and the AAA. This led to the October 1994 approval of the full $500,000 by the Sponsor's Task Force.

Building on groundwork laid by the AECC, the Educational Advisory Committee of the AAA developed a strategic approach to faculty development, and the AAA hired Dr. Tracey E. Sutherland to implement the program. I have been impressed with the AAA's activities in faculty development. Although the full impact of the AAA's efforts is not yet clear, there are many promising signs. For example, continuing education sessions at both national and regional AAA meetings have grown quickly. At the 1990 AAA Annual Meeting there were 21 continuing education sessions preceding the meetings that attracted 691 participants. By 1998 this had grown to 33 sessions with 919 participants. The lasting impact of the AECC's activities, especially achieving continuous change and improvements in accounting education, depends greatly on the success of the AAA's faculty development effort.

The last half of the Commission's life was less exciting than the first half, but the activities were essential to its success. The scope of its activities was more limited, and there was less creating and more implementing. But if the later activities had not been undertaken with dedication and enthusiasm, the early gains might have been lost. It is to the credit of the Commission members and leadership that no momentum was lost, and the hand-off to the AAA of ongoing activities, primarily faculty development, was smooth.

Stewardship

In total, the sponsoring firms pledged $5 million to support the seven-year life of the AECC. Of course, the major portion of the support was for the grant program. However, the Commission also used the funds for its other activities. The $5 million was invested as follows:

Grant program, including direct payments to 13 colleges and universities	$3.0 million
Dissemination of AECC work products, including workshops, publications, presentations, etc.	.5
Administrative expenses, including compensation to AECC Chairs and Executive Directors, meetings expenses, and office expenses	1.5
Total	$5.0 million

The support of the sponsoring firms was essential for the success of the Commission. Nevertheless, $5 million is only a fraction of the cost of the needed changes. As Barefield (1991, 310) pointed out, "IBM's effort to develop MIS curricula cost more than $10 million and the effort was focused on a much smaller academic discipline." The AECC and the accounting academy in general had to highly leverage these funds to gain improvements across a majority of the accounting programs in the country. The grant schools provided leverage through matching funds, but the real leverage came from convincing colleges and universities to undertake change activities without external funding. Several of the programs doing so were described in the special AECC issues of *Accounting Education News* (see chapter 5). The Commission may have been a catalyst for some of these changes, but without the leadership of a number of schools and individuals around the country, the change effort would not have succeeded.

Chapter 4
THE GRANT PROGRAM

Because of the high respect for the members of the Commission throughout its life, positions taken by the Commission were sure to receive attention. But money speaks louder than words, and the Commission's grant program attracted the most notice. About 60 percent of the Commission's initial $4 million budget was set aside for grants to colleges and universities that proposed significant changes in their accounting programs.

The Commission was authorized to make grants by the following provisions of the Memorandum of Understanding:

1) The Commission is authorized to award grants to departments or schools of accounting, colleges, and universities subject to the following limitations:
   a) All grants must be intended to further the Objectives and AAA Charge.
   b) Grants should be directed to achieve the broadest possible impact upon the programs of the recipient institutions. Evidence of institutional support and/or concurrent authorization for a specific proposal is desirable. Grants should not be awarded to individuals.
   c) The maximum grant to a single institution shall be $250,000.
   d) Grants shall not fund institutional overhead.
2) The Commission shall offer grants on a competitive basis, shall determine grant criteria, publish and broadly disseminate a grant prospectus setting forth the proposal requirements and grant criteria, establish a deadline for the receipt of proposals, evaluate and rank proposals, negotiate terms with selected proposers, and enter into grant contracts. Such contracts shall provide for percentage-of-completion payments, based upon clearly defined benchmarks with a retainage of at least 10 percent until successful completion of the grant terms.
3) The Commission shall monitor grants to encourage successful outcomes.

At the Commission's first meeting, two of these provisions were questioned. First, several members felt that innovation more often comes from individuals than from institutions. Further, they believed that certain types of schools would not be able to develop buy-in by an entire faculty, thereby prohibiting participation in the grant program. Thus, they wanted to set aside a small percentage of the available funds for grants to individuals. The Commission decided that the focus on *implementation* of changes required institutional commitment, and therefore restricting grants to institutions was appropriate. Second, some questioned the restriction on paying overhead because it would preclude smaller schools from applying. Because making exceptions would jeopardize the overhead-free arrangements with other institutions, the Commission agreed with the no-overhead clause. The other provisions were accepted without extensive discussion.

Issuing the Request for Proposals

The Commission moved quickly in setting up the grant program. Before the Commission's first meeting, the Executive Director was instructed to prepare a draft Request For Proposals (RFP). At the first meeting the RFP was revised, and on November 1, 1989, the RFP was approved. It was mailed on November 20, with a submission date for proposals of February 1, 1990. At the same meeting the Commission announced a second round of submissions due December 1, 1990.

This speed was criticized by Barefield (1991, 310):

> The AECC moved too quickly to implement its grants program....[T]he full academic community was not adequately involved in the program....Under these conditions, 10 weeks is too short a time period to allow for the full development of "sweeping change" proposals.

He also criticized the selection procedure because it did not include a site visit before making a grant, a process that would also have slowed down the process. While the Commission's operating procedures allowed for site visits if needed, no site visits were undertaken.

Barefield's (1991) criticisms had some validity. The first round of grants was biased in favor of schools that had already put thought into program revisions. Many major accounting programs elected to not submit proposals rather than submit ones that were not fully developed. This was mitigated somewhat by the second round when several highly ranked programs submitted proposals. Nevertheless, programs tended to be left out of the process if they had not started to develop program revisions and were so large that quickly gaining faculty consensus was difficult. Further, the absence of site visits limited the Commission's ability to judge the extent of commitment to the proposal and the ability to successfully implement it. With hindsight, I believe that fewer than 20 percent of the grants would have gone to different programs if site visits had been included.

The Request For Proposals is shown in its entirety in exhibit 4-1. It was mailed to Presidents and Business School Deans of AACSB-member schools and to all Accounting Department Heads and Deans of Schools of Accountancy identified in the 1989 *Accounting Faculty Directory*. The most significant provisions of the RFP were:

- Proposed changes must be consistent with the Bedford Committee report and the Big 8 White Paper. Although Barefield (1991, 309), among others, believed that that the White Paper was "too...untested a foundation on which to build sweeping educational change," the Commission never wavered in its application of this criterion.
- Preference was given to proposals for comprehensive change throughout the curriculum and proposals for changes in individual courses were discouraged. The Commission believed that past attempts at changing the introductory accounting curriculum failed because the changes did not affect upper-level accounting courses.
- Proposals had to include a plan to measure the success of the project. This proved to be an elusive goal, and the Commission devoted special attention to the issue as described in chapter 8.
- Program changes should be transferable to other institutions. This criterion was one of the main factors separating the more successful grant projects from the less successful.
- The institution should show commitment to the project, preferably by cost sharing. To achieve maximum benefit from limited funds, the Commission tried to leverage its dollars.

In examining the distribution list for the RFP, it became clear to the Commission that one important type of institution had been ignored—the two-year colleges. The immediate solution was to encourage four-year schools to partner with two-year schools when submitting proposals. As discussed later, a further response was to solicit proposals from two-year schools in a separate round of funding.

Selection of Proposals for Funding

The first-round request for proposals generated 40 applications. The Commission's objective was to grant no more than one-half of the available funds on the first round. Requests for funding ranged from under $100,000 to the $250,000 maximum.

A screening committee consisting of the Commission Chairman, Executive Director, and four other Commission members evaluated all proposals. The committee divided proposals into three

---

EXHIBIT 4-1
Accounting Education Change Commission

REQUEST FOR PROPOSALS

The Accounting Education Change Commission (AECC) announces a program to award grants to departments or schools of accounting, colleges, and universities. The purpose of the grant program is to foster changes in the academic preparation of accountants consistent with the goal of improving their capabilities for successful professional accounting careers. These capabilities are described in the Sponsoring Firms' White Paper, *Perspectives on Education: Capabilities for Success in the Accounting Profession*, and in the American Accounting Association report of the Committee on the Future Structure, Content and Scope of Accounting Education, both of which are available upon request from the Executive Director of AECC.

The total amount available for AECC grant programs over the five-year life of the Commission is slightly over $2 million. It is generally expected that not more than $1 million will be granted on the first round.

1) Proposals for the first round of funding should be submitted by February 1, 1990. Proposals for the second round will be due December 1, 1990. Five (5) copies of the proposal should be submitted to:

> Gary L. Sundem, Executive Director
> Accounting Education Change Commission
> 365 Ericksen Avenue NE, Suite 327
> Bainbridge Island, WA 98110

2) The full proposal should be accompanied by an executive summary of no more than 3 pages. The maximum length of proposals, including appendices, should be 50 pages.

3) Proposals must be endorsed by departments or schools of accounting, colleges, or universities, and the appropriate academic officer. Official institutional support of the proposal should be described in the application. Proposals from a consortium of two or more institutions are acceptable; such proposals must have the endorsement of all involved institutions.

4) A project leader should be identified and the roles of all participants in the project should be specified. Qualifications, including relevant experience, of all individuals involved in the proposed project should be provided as part of the proposal.

5) Projects may extend well beyond one year. Therefore, proposals should break the total project into phases and allocate the requested funding to phases. Payments will be made on completion of each phase. Progress payments will be equal to 90 percent of the funds allocated to the completed phase; the remaining 10 percent will be paid upon completion of the entire project. Proposals must contain target dates for completing each phase of the project.

6) Not more than $250,000 will be granted to any one project or any one college or university.

7) Grants shall not fund institutional overhead.

Grant proposals will be judged on their potential to foster desirable changes in the academic preparation of accountants. Grants are for IMPLEMENTING CHANGES. Proposals must address action plans for implementation; further study of curriculum changes is insufficient. Among the guidelines used to judge proposals are:

Purpose of the Projects

- Goals and Objectives. Proposals shall have goals and objectives consistent with the recommendations of the *Report of the AAA Committee on the Future Content, Structure and Scope of Accounting Education* and *Perspectives on Education: Capabilities for Success in the Accounting Profession*.
- Potential for Success. Projects will be evaluated on the potential for the proposed activities to successfully accomplish the desired changes in the recipient institution(s).

Description and Scope

- Description of Project Details. The project should be described in enough detail to allow an evaluation of its potential effectiveness. The description should include a discussion of the improvements sought and the proposed methods of achieving the project's objectives.

(Continued on next page)

EXHIBIT 4-1 (Continued)

- Breadth of Potential Impact. Proposals for comprehensive changes in the academic program are preferred to proposals to implement changes in only portions of the curriculum. Proposals relating to single courses are discouraged.
- Creativity. Creative, innovative approaches will enhance a proposal's ranking.

Desired Results

- Measurement of Success. Proposals should include methods for assessing the success of proposed changes. Recipients of grants should be willing to participate in broad measures of success that might be developed by the Commission.
- Transferability of Changes. The potential use of curriculum changes by other institutions is important. Proposals should address the potential for such transferability.
- Dissemination of Results. Proposals should include plans for communicating the results of the change activities to others, possibly including publications, symposia, conference presentations, etc.

Strategies and Timeline of Implementation

- Implementation Strategy. Proposals should include a strategy for implementing proposed changes. Evaluation will include an assessment of the efficiency of the strategy.
- Timing. Proposals with early implementation activities have priority over proposals with delayed implementation.

Budget and Commitment

- Benefit/Cost. Proposals promising the greatest potential benefit per dollar of funding have priority.
- Cost sharing. Proposals that include cost sharing, for example partial financial support such as release time from the institution, have higher priority.
- Institutional Commitment. A proposal's rank will be enhanced if it includes evidence that the administration of the proposing institution is committed to implementation of academic changes and will reward project participants for successful curriculum innovations.

The Commission will announce grant recipients by March 15, 1990. Executive summaries of winning proposals will be made available to the public.

---

categories: (1) those recommended for funding, (2) a set of proposals equal in dollar amount to those recommended for funding consisting of the highest ranked proposals not recommended for funding, and (3) the remaining proposals not recommended for funding. The proposals in the first two categories were ranked, and a summary evaluation of every proposal was prepared. Commission members received executive summaries for all proposals and full proposals for any they requested. Proposals receiving a majority favorable vote of the Commission were funded.

To avoid conflicts of interest, Commission members refrained from participation in the development of proposals and did not participate in discussion or votes on any proposal in which it might be perceived that they had a personal interest. In addition, no one with a personal interest in any submitted project could be on the screening committee.

From the 40 submitted proposals, five were selected for funding: Brigham Young University, Kansas State University, University of Massachusetts Amherst, University of North Texas, and Rutgers University. AECC funding supplied an average of 35 percent of the resources required for these projects:

University	Total Budget	AECC Funding in $	% AECC Funding
Brigham Young	$ 435,000	$250,000	57%
Kansas State	384,000	249,500	65
Massachusetts	400,588	93,400	23
North Texas	1,057,034	243,198	19
Rutgers	501,500	140,500	28
Total	$2,778,122	$976,598	35%

Fifty proposals were submitted by December 1, 1990 for the second round of funding. Using the same procedure as in the first round, the Commission selected five projects involving six universities: Arizona State University, University of Chicago, Universities of Illinois and Notre Dame (the only grant to a joint project involving two universities), North Carolina A&T State University, and University of Virginia. The $1.16 million granted in the second round brought the total of the grants to approximately $2.14 million:

University	Total Budget	AECC Funding in $	% AECC Funding
Arizona State	$650,000	$250,000	38%
Chicago	442,000	196,000	44
Illinois/Notre Dame	3,249,803	300,000	9
North Carolina A&T	297,000	165,000	56
Virginia	833,000	250,000	30
Net Total	$5,471,803	$1,161,000	21%

The final phase of the grant program was grants to two-year colleges. The request for proposals with a submission deadline of January 15, 1992 had two main changes from that in exhibit 4-1. First, grants had a maximum amount of $50,000 to any institution. Second, the grants were for "the academic preparation of students planning to transfer to accounting programs in four-year institutions." The breadth-of-potential-impact criterion was amended as follows:

> Breadth of potential impact. Proposals should focus on the introductory accounting courses, commonly called principles of accounting but sometimes offered as separate financial and managerial accounting courses. However, other courses offered to transfer students may also be included in the proposal. Special attention should be given to articulation of transfer credits. Projects focused on teaching methods as well as curriculum content are encouraged.

Two grants totaling $92,000 were made, one to Kirkwood Community College and one to Mesa Community College:

Two-Year College	Total Budget	AECC Funding in $	% AECC Funding
Kirkwood	$100,699	$50,000	50%
Mesa	82,500	42,000	51
Total	$183,199	$92,000	50%

Characteristics of Funded Projects

I will not discuss the individual grant projects in this monograph. Descriptions of the original proposals were published in *Issues in Accounting Education* (Williams and Sundem 1990, 1991; Williams 1992c). Completed project summaries are in a monograph by Flaherty (1998). However, I will discuss some of the characteristics that elevated the funded proposals above those that were not funded. All of the characteristics apply to the four-year schools, and all but the breadth or comprehensiveness characteristics apply to the two-year schools.

All proposals represented improvements to the accounting program at the proposer's institution. The funded proposals promised benefits beyond the improvement of that one program. In addition, the funded proposals tended to be more comprehensive than were the others. The addition of a communications component or case studies to an existing curriculum was often an element of a successful proposal, but such changes alone, without changing the basic philosophy and structure of the curriculum, did not provide a model for the major changes needed in accounting education.

Successful proposals also integrated changes throughout the curriculum. Proposals focusing on a narrow part of the accounting curriculum were not funded. Restructuring the curriculum to focus on information and information systems, as recommended by the Bedford Committee, was a definite plus. Another element regarded favorably in evaluating proposals was integration with the liberal arts curriculum. In hindsight, I think this factor was overrated, as explained in chapter 6.

Two factors that were weighed in the decision, but on which few proposals were strong, were creativity and outcome measurement. In a sense, all proposals were innovative because they were new to the proposing institution. Further, some proposals had creative elements. However, creativity in terms of truly new approaches to accounting education was not abundant. Similarly, ways of measuring the success of implemented changes were included in all funded projects, but it seemed that, for many of the proposals, outcome measurement was an afterthought that was added just because the request for proposals required it. As a result, the Commission itself took the lead in developing appropriate outcome measures and procedures.

A final factor was essential to the success of the proposals—institutional support. An accounting faculty that was widely involved in and fully committed to change and strong endorsements by deans and higher university officials were deemed necessary for successful implementation of changes. Substantial but realistic financial commitments by the institution were helpful, but not as essential as faculty buy-in. Judging this area may have benefited from site visits, especially for unsuccessful proposals where it seemed that there was little buy-in, but where the fault might have been in proposal preparation and not in actual fact.

Grant Program Success

The grant schools were essentially engaged in research and development projects. In research activities, one expects more failures than successes. However, almost all grant projects accomplished a majority of the desired changes in the grant school's program. The reports from the grant schools make it clear that none would prefer to go back to the program that was in place before the changes. Either the grant projects were more like development than research projects, or they had a phenomenal success rate. I believe the former. There are two things that would have made these real research projects. First would be undertaking changes that truly had unknown impacts, and second would be process research, illustrating how to accomplish the process of change. The grant projects had little of the former. The jury is still out on the latter, but we might find that the improvements are not widespread or that they are only a minor part of the improvements needed to guarantee the viability of accounting programs into the twenty-first century.

It is too early to develop conclusive evidence about whether graduates from the grant schools' programs are better prepared for professional accounting careers than were earlier graduates or graduates from other colleges and universities. However, I think it is unlikely that we will find that the changes did not result in improvements in the grant schools' programs. Evidence from early output measures such as exit interviews is encouraging, as is anecdotal evidence from employers. However, success in important areas such as ability to adapt to change will take years to assess. Therefore, I am willing to accept a verdict of initial success and good prospects for long-term success in developing the types of graduates who will succeed in the accounting profession.

If the contribution of the grant projects were to illustrate what does and does not work in the *process* of implementing change, we would expect widespread imitation of the change processes that work. However, transfer of changes from grant schools to others has been slower than some anticipated. On the positive side, some transfers are taking place. Significant changes have occurred or are occurring in a majority of accounting programs, so it may be that the influence of the experiences of the grant schools is subtle. Few schools are adopting wholesale the revised programs at the grant schools. However, materials developed from the grant projects, such as the Ainsworth (1996) textbook and the Smith and Birney (1995) software, are being widely used. In addition, elements of programs, such as the integration of accounting and information systems at Brigham Young University, the moving of technical accounting subjects to a computer lab as at Arizona State University, and the addition of group work and communication modules in several programs, are being incorporated into many accounting programs. There is little doubt that the grant projects are affecting other programs, but they are not yet the full prototypes that some envisioned.

Most of the transferable results of the grant projects relate to delivery methods. Changes such as a user orientation, increased emphasis on critical thinking and communication skills, and altering the order in which topics are taught (including integration of topics) were relatively uncontroversial. The main argument against any of these was a cost/benefit one—what must be given up in order to achieve these objectives. One reason that the grant projects were locally successful is that most of them addressed primarily these delivery-method issues. They did not tackle the most difficult changes advocated by the Bedford Committee, changes in the basic nature of the subjects included in an accounting curriculum.

The Big 8 White Paper, which focused primarily on teaching and learning methods, had a more limited focus than the Bedford Committee report, which also advocated changes in the definition of accounting. Most grant projects addressed issues in the White Paper. Nearly all projects dodged the Bedford Committee's redefinition of accounting as a "broad economic information development and distribution process, based on the design, implementation, and operation of multiple types of information systems." (AAA 1986, 185) They did not address the Bedford Committee's view that the "accounting profession will provide information for economic and social decisions, using sophisticated measurement and communication technologies applied to a substantially enlarged scope of phenomena." (AAA 1986, 171) To address these issues would require more fundamental changes in the accounting curriculum and instructional materials than occurred in the grant programs. Whether such changes can successfully be built into an accounting curriculum remains an open question.

I do not want to imply that none of the projects attempted to address the changing definition of accounting. Brigham Young University and Arizona State University elevated the position of information systems in the accounting curriculum, ASU primarily by moving it before financial reporting in the sequence of courses and BYU by using an information systems framework for the entire curriculum. The Universities of Illinois and Notre Dame developed an approach that leads to a better conceptual understanding of accounting and therefore a better ability to adapt to changes in the accounting profession. Others also touched on smaller elements of this issue. But even in these projects, more fundamental changes are necessary if the accounting profession is to continue down the path proposed by the Bedford Committee.

Lessons From the Change Process

As indicated in the previous section, most of the lessons learned from the grant projects related to teaching (and learning) methods. Most widespread success was incorporating a user orientation, especially in the introductory courses but also in more advanced courses as well. Most of the projects also included an increased emphasis on communication skills, primarily written but also oral. Without exception, these efforts were deemed to be successful. The addition of team experiences, active learning, and cooperative learning components were also generally judged to be successful. The only caveats related to the difficulty of accomplishing these objectives in large-sized classes and the problems encountered when extending the concept of team exercises to team or group grading.

Attempts to make the curriculum more conceptual, with a reduced emphasis on techniques, rules, and regulations, worked well, most directly at the Universities of Illinois and Notre Dame but indirectly at several other grant schools. More case method teaching was also successful in several projects. Finally, using textbooks as references rather than as the central focus of the course was mentioned as a desirable change by several programs.

Interestingly, in the final project reports, only one school, the University of Illinois, touted its assessment program as a success that others should copy. An excellent article about the University of Illinois' assessment was published in the *Journal of Accounting Research* (Stone and Shelley 1997). Although assessment was not the strongest part of most projects, I think there are things to emulate in other projects' assessment measures, especially those used by Brigham Young University.

On a negative side, the most frequent comment was that the costs and efforts involved in the change process greatly exceeded what was anticipated. Not only did the change process take a great deal of faculty time, the newly implemented teaching methods also were more faculty-time-intensive than old methods. Projects such as that at Arizona State University explicitly tried to address this by replacing faculty time with technology in areas where this was feasible. However, in all the projects, any resources made available by restructuring were quickly consumed in resource-intensive aspects of the new curriculum.

Summary

The grant program was the springboard that propelled the AECC into an undeniable force on the accounting landscape. Without the ability to make grants, the Commission would have been simply a blue-ribbon committee with much influence on those already committed to change but little influence on the average accounting program. However, both the symbolism of financial support and the possibility of participating in funded curriculum change caught the attention of most accounting faculty.

After less than three years of existence, the Commission was recognized by 97 percent of a sample of deans, department chairs, and senior faculty from top-ranked accounting programs and by more than 91 percent of a random sample of accounting faculty.[6] Without the grant program, this recognition would not have been possible. Therefore, the grant program was probably responsible for more changes in accounting education than those changes directly attributable to the grant projects.

The grant projects had many positive impacts, but their enduring effect is still unknown. They were less adventuresome than hoped, but dedicated leaders and faculty made all the projects successful in some way. Every accounting faculty member who reads the summary of the grant projects in Flaherty (1998) will learn something useful for their classes and their programs. It is unlikely that a single prototype will serve as a model program, but elements of the projects are sure to stimulate ideas for improvement.

---

[6]   See Ehrenreich and Hulme (1992).

Chapter 5
PROMOTING CHANGE

The AECC's mandate was to be a catalyst for change throughout all accounting education programs. If all of the grant projects were successful at the grantee institutions but they had no effect on other programs, the Commission would be judged a failure. The goal was to engage all programs in the dialogue for change and encourage each to change in a way that best meets its mission.

To achieve widespread changes, the Commission focused much of its attention on promoting change. In the early years this consisted primarily of convincing constituencies of the need for change and establishing the types of changes needed. In the last half of the Commission's life, it spent more time providing guidance on how to change.

The Commission itself summarized its activities promoting change in the annual reports prepared after each of its first four years. Unfortunately, it ceased preparing annual reports after that, so summarized information on the last three years is not available.

Selling the Need for Change

Most of the presentations and publications by members of the Commission were directed toward selling the need for change. As part of this, they included the main directions for change as summarized in AECC Position Statement No. One, *Objectives of Education for Accountants*. Later promotion efforts focusing on implementing change fell primarily to the grant schools, although the Commission provided forums and otherwise facilitated such presentations and publications.

Promotion activities included official Commission initiatives and activities undertaken by individual Commission members. The official initiatives included the following: (1) published the official Statements of the Commission, (2) summarized the AECC meetings in issues of *Accounting Education News*, (3) published five special issues of *Accounting Education News*, (3) published four annual reports of Commission activities, (4) held five workshops and symposia, (5) distributed materials to stakeholders, and (6) arranged panels and presentations at scores of professional meetings. The first of these is covered in chapter 6, and the rest will be discussed later in this chapter.

In the Commission's first four years, individual members made about 320 presentations to audiences numbering nearly 30,000. In addition, more than 20 articles about accounting education change written by Commission members were published through mid-1993. Among the journals in which they appeared are *The Journal of Accountancy*, *Management Accounting*, *IMA Campus Reports*, *Issues in Accounting Education*, *Accounting Education*, *The Accounting Educator*, *New Accountant*, and *Today's CPA*.

The Commission also distributed many documents to a variety of stakeholders. Issues Statement No. 1 received the widest exposure, including a mailing to Chairs of Boards of Trustees (or Regents) of colleges and universities. The Boyer (1990) report, *Scholarship Reconsidered: Priorities for the Professoriate*, was sent to all accounting department chairs. The Commission sent all its official Statements to deans and accounting department chairs, and it sent several of them to higher university administrators.

The promotion efforts of the Commission did not go unnoticed. A survey in early 1992 (Ehrenreich and Hulme 1992) found that 97 percent of a select sample of deans, accounting department chairs, and senior faculty from top-rated schools had heard of the AECC, as had 91 percent of a random sample of accounting faculty. The message was also getting across, with 90 percent of the former group and 86 percent of the latter indicating a need for moderate to major change in accounting education. The effectiveness of the Commission in carrying the message was not as clear cut, with 62 percent of the select group and 58 percent of the random group having a favorable to very favorable impression of the AECC's activities. However, only 10 percent and 12 percent of the respondents were disappointed or very disappointed with the AECC's efforts.

By the end of its third year, the Commission realized that complacency, or lack of recognition of the need to change, was no longer the main impediment to change. Rather, it was lack of knowledge of how to change and lack of resources to implement the needed changes. The last four years of the Commission's life were devoted mostly to disseminating information on how to change accounting programs, derived mainly from the experiences of the grant schools.

Publications in *Accounting Education News*

The AECC published summaries of its meetings in *Accounting Education News* (*AEN*). The meetings were held in various parts of the country and observers were welcome at the meetings, but only about eight or ten observers were usually present. Thus, to keep the activities of the Commission open and known to anyone interested, meeting summaries were made widely available. Minutes were sent to anyone requesting to be on the mailing list. But most effective were the meeting summaries in *AEN*.

In addition to the meeting summaries, the AECC produced five special issues of *Accounting Education News*. These issues had three main topics: (1) information about the AECC's activities in general, (2) descriptions of the findings from the grant projects, and (3) descriptions of change activities at nongrant colleges and universities.

The first special issue in June 1990 highlighted the proposed changes at the first five grant schools. It also included changes being undertaken at the University of Alberta, the University of Idaho, and the University of Southern California. Finally, it contained the request for proposals for the second round of grants, together with a description of what distinguished the grants that were successful in the first round.

The successful grant proposals from the second round were described in the 1991 special issue, together with change activities at Adrian College, the University of Florida, and Michigan State University. Also included was a summary of the "Symposium on Models of Accounting Education."

The 1992 and 1993 special issues of *AEN* included the proposed changes at the two-year colleges that received grants and several articles describing aspects of the change process:

- Description of program changes underway at California State University, Chico, including Curt DeBerg's use of a student journal to encourage development of writing skills
- An overview of the award-winning management accounting course developed by Sherry Mills and Cathleen Burns at New Mexico State University
- John DeNicolo's comparison of the "new age" accounting principles course with the traditional approach
- Curriculum changes at Florida International University
- A summary of methods used to recruit accounting students compiled by the AECC Student Quality Task Force

- Reprint of an article on assessing student learning form *Principles of Good Practice for Assessing Student Learning*, published by the American Association for Higher Education
- Recommendations for those considering curriculum changes by Jay Smith based on his experiences with the Brigham Young University grant project
- Donald Brown's description of a new Introduction to Accounting course at Brock University. That is appropriate where curriculum development resources are limited
- A description by Jeff Harkins of how an accounting course can focus on the development of critical-thinking skills
- Suggestions by Phillip Korb and Gail Wright on how to change accounting textbooks to incorporate AECC objectives

Finally, the 1994 special issue was devoted primarily to progress updates and findings from 11 of the 12 grant projects. It included contact information for the project leaders of all grant projects for anyone who wanted more information about any of the projects.

Workshops and Symposia

The Commission sponsored five self-standing workshops or symposia in addition to many workshops in connection with AAA annual or regional meetings. The first of these focused on the need for change and how to start the change process. The other four addressed findings from the grant projects.

The "Symposium on Models of Accounting Education," co-sponsored with the Education Advisory Committee of the AAA, was held in Dallas, Texas on March 8–9, 1991. After planning for an attendance of 70, the response was so great that more than 200 participants, the physical capacity of the facility, were accommodated. Each session was presented twice, each time to an audience of about 100. Because department chairs were invited to nominate only one person from their college or university, a broad spectrum of schools was represented. The program committee of Fred Streuling, Milton Usry, and Tom Williams of the Education Advisory Committee and Jim Loebbecke, Corine Norgaard, Gary Sundem, and Doyle Williams of the AECC selected the following eight papers for presentation:

- *Reals and Ideals of Accounting Education: Building Educational Leverages on Fundamentals*, Y. Ijiri and S. Sunder
- *A Model of Undergraduate Accounting Education for Life-Long Learning*, G. S. Smith and C. Smith
- *Student Capabilities and Instructional Methods: A Framework for Curriculum Development, Assessment, and Research*, L. Rankin
- *A Comprehensive Model for Accounting Education*, B. Needles, Jr. and H. Anderson
- *Accounting 2000: The First Year*, L. Malgeri and D. Brawley
- *The Role of Information Technology and Information Systems Knowledge in the Accounting Curriculum*, J. Kinard
- *The Role of Doctoral Programs in the Improvement of Accounting Education*, R. Ingram
- *Education for the "Profession" of Accounting,* J. Wheeler

Doyle Williams and Rene Manes gave talks at dinner and lunch, respectively. The program was very well received, especially by those just contemplating or in the early stages of curriculum changes. The program's weakness, as noted primarily by those who had given a great deal of thought to accounting program changes, was the lack of truly innovative approaches to change. The Commission published and distributed the proceedings of the symposium (Norgaard and Sundem 1991).

After this first symposium, the Commission decided that the cost of further broad-based symposia designed to get schools started on program changes was greater than its value. Instead, the Commission directed future resources to workshops on implementation issues.

In January 1994, Brigham Young University hosted a workshop where two grant schools, BYU and Kansas State University, shared their curriculum change experiences with 52 administrators and colleagues from 26 other colleges and universities. The program included model classroom sessions, extensive analysis of the process of planning and implementing curriculum changes, and assessments of the changes by student groups. Feedback from the participants was very positive, indicating that these two grant projects have many elements that are transferable to other programs.

About a year later, in February 1995, an "Introduction to Accounting Workshop" was held in Tempe, Arizona. The Commission received more than twice as many applications to attend as could be accommodated. About 170 participants from a wide variety of colleges and universities, including several two-year colleges, were very pleased with the program developed primarily by Rich Flaherty and Mel O'Connor. They heard about the introductory accounting courses at the following colleges and universities (with presenters):

University of Alabama—R. Ingram
University of Alabama at Birmingham—T. Edmonds
Arizona State University—R. Birney and K. Jones
California State University, Chico—C. DeBerg
University of Illinois—A. Feller
Kansas State University—P. Ainsworth and D. Deines
Kirkwood Community College—M. Tharp and J. Zeller
Massachusetts Institute of Technology—P. Wilson
Mesa Community College—A. Ormiston
Michigan State University—A. Arens
University of Notre Dame—T. Frecka, T. Mittelstaedt, and R. Ramanan
University of Southern California—K. Pincus
University of Virginia—D. Scott

As one example of the impact of this workshop, Bob Eskew of Purdue University wrote the following (excerpted) to Richard Flaherty three months after the workshop:

> I want you to know that the AECC program I attended in Phoenix in February has had an impact at Purdue. I was intrigued by Al Arens' explanation of what they had done at MSU [Michigan State University]. I followed up with a phone call....I visited MSU....On the basis of that information, I proposed that we offer an experimental section of our introductory course this fall using the MSU approach modified to fit our circumstances....Thanks to you and the AECC for putting on a program that is responsible for what is likely to be a significant change (improvement) in how we deliver introductory accounting. (Eskew 1995)

In its last year, the Commission sponsored two workshops. The first was held October 17–18, 1996 at the University of Illinois. It focused on Project Discovery, the Illinois/Notre Dame AECC grant project. It was essentially a "how-to" conference for schools that wanted to implement parts of Project Discovery.

The second workshop, "Measuring the Path of Excellence: What Works Well in Accounting Education," focused on assessment and was held on the University of Notre Dame campus on May 29–31, 1997. It explored setting a program's mission and objectives, measuring progress toward those objectives, and modifying the program accordingly. It looked at assessment of courses, both during and after the course, as well as assessment of the entire curriculum. In essence, it put assessment in the context of continuous improvement of accounting programs.

Another workshop, the "Conference on Teaching" held at the University of Notre Dame in June 1991, was influenced by, though not sponsored by, the AECC. The conference proceedings (Frecka 1992) indicate that the conference was "in support of Project Discovery, the joint University of Illinois/University of Notre Dame Accounting Curriculum Development Project." This conference focused on critical thinking, active learning, and technology. Most of the presenters were experts from fields other than accounting. The papers presented were not about Project Discovery; rather, they related to concepts and methods that were inputs to the design of Project Discovery. As such, the proceedings are useful to any faculty wanting to enhance the critical thinking and active learning components of their curriculum.

Videotapes

The Commission produced two well-received videotapes. The first was directed toward convincing faculty of the need for changes and pointing out the directions of that change. The second focused on how to make some of the needed pedagogical changes.

At the 1991 AAA Annual Meeting, the AECC sponsored a plenary session that was taped by Arthur Andersen & Co., which was widely distributed by the Commission. Charles Nessen, Professor of Law at Harvard University, moderated a panel discussion about changes in accounting education. The panel included:

- William H. Beaver, Professor, Stanford University
- Ray J. Groves, Co-Chief Executive, Ernst & Young
- William Livingstone, Vice President, University of Texas at Austin
- Gerhard G. Mueller, Professor, University of Washington
- Stanley A. Pylipow, Senior Vice President and CFO, Fisher Controls International
- A. Marvin Strait, Chairman of the Board, Strait, Kushinsky & Co.
- Richard R. West, Dean, Stern School of Business, New York University

The discussion focused first on the need for reform in accounting education. All panelists agreed on the need for changes. However, there were differences in opinion on the types and degree of changes. The first half of the 90-minute program dealt mainly with defining the problems as perceived by both practitioners and academics. The second half focused more on reasons that students are not as well prepared for professional accounting careers as they could be and what might be done to remedy this. Two areas receiving special attention were the performance evaluation and reward systems for faculty and the role of accreditation in promoting or stifling change. The discussion is entertaining as well as enlightening.

The impetus for the second videotape came from efforts to develop a symposium on teaching skills. Because of the limited exposure of a symposium, the Commission decided to instead develop a videotape that could be viewed by more faculty than could attend a symposium. The program was developed and presented by Professors Tomas R. Dyckman and G. Peter Wilson. Taping took place at the 1992 AAA New Faculty Consortium sponsored by Arthur Andersen & Co. Dyckman spoke on "Teaching Effectively via Discussion and Seminars," and Wilson addressed "Teaching: Structuring and Communicating Knowledge." The videotape continues to have great relevance, and I highly recommend it to anyone trying to improve his or her teaching. It would be especially helpful to Ph.D. students who are preparing for faculty careers.

Panels and Presentations

Much more promotion of the AECC and its activities occurred at the meetings of other organizations than through the Commission's symposium and workshops. The major vehicle for reaching accounting academics was the meetings of the American Accounting Association (AAA). From 1990 through the end of its life, the Commission sponsored sessions at every regional and national AAA Annual Meeting. Commission members made many luncheon and dinner speeches, in addition to plenary and concurrent sessions. In addition, there were presentations about educational change at most other meetings such as the New Faculty Consortium, the Doctoral Consortium, and the annual meeting of the Administrators of Accounting Programs Group.

Other academic organizations, such as the Federation of Schools of Accountancy, generally included the Commission on their annual meeting programs. Most years there was a session on accounting education change at the AACSB annual meeting. In addition to presentations at organized conferences, there were many presentations on campuses, sometimes to the faculty of a single university and often to faculty from several universities in the area.

Commission members also made presentations at a variety of international universities and academic accounting conferences, as described later in this chapter. Although extension of the Commission's activities to an international audience was not a major objective, it was clear that there was great international interest in the Commission's success.

The nature of the presentations changed as the Commission aged. As with publications and workshops, the focus on rallying support for change in the early years (with Commission members delivering much of the message) evolved to a focus on methods of change in the later years (with faculty at grant schools bearing much of the burden). Each of the grant schools made an average of about 20 presentations about its project.

Presentations at nonacademic meetings were more limited. Professional accounting organizations such as FEI and IMA supported the Commission's activities but provided little opportunity for presentations on their annual meeting programs; most presentations were to committees or boards of these organizations. One organization that was more receptive to Commission presentations was the National Association of State Boards of Accountancy, with presentations at least once to all regional annual meetings. The AICPA provided opportunities for the Commission on programs directed toward academics, but not often on programs directed toward practitioners. Some state CPA societies provided a forum for presentations, and several major accounting firms invited Commission members to address their partners and/or recruiting personnel. Although the number of presentations to practitioner groups was reasonably large, the large size of the potential audience made reaching even a moderate percentage of practitioners difficult.

AECC Monographs

To help colleges and universities deal with two of the most difficult aspects of the change process, the Commission published two commissioned monographs. The first monograph was on accounting program assessment (Gainen and Locatelli 1995), which is covered in more detail in chapter 8. The second was on intentional learning (Francis et al. 1995), an expansion on the concept of "learning to learn," which is a major component of life-long learning and a concept central to the objectives of the Commission. It will be described in this section.

Both monographs were written by national experts in the field with assistance from Commission co-authors and advisory/review boards. Both were designed to provide practical help to accounting departments, not to simply provide general guidelines. Further, both monographs received strong positive reviews from outside reviewers. Gerry Mueller concluded that the monographs "are likely to become educational tools in academic accounting departments nationwide" (Mueller 1995). I think it is significant that these monographs were published under the auspices of both the AECC and the AAA as part of the AAA Educational Monograph Series, signifying that these ideas should not die with the Commission but should be carried forward by the faculty development efforts of the AAA.

Shortly after the Commission took a strong position advocating "learning to learn" as a major component of accounting programs, it received several requests to elaborate on the concept and to provide guidelines on how to achieve such a goal. With the guidance of Joan Stark and Jim Loebbecke, the Commission oversaw the publication of *Intentional Learning: A Process for Learning to Learn in the Accounting Curriculum* (Francis et al. 1995). In the words of the authors, the monograph does the following:

It begins with a description of accountants as learners and professionals, and presents a definition of and perspectives on learning to learn. The second chapter introduces a new concept—the intentional learning process—and the attributes of intentional learning as a manageable approach to teaching students to be independent learners. The third chapter presents characteristics of learners that influence their attitudes toward learning and their ability to learn. The fourth chapter discusses the learning process and teaching strategies that can encourage students to learn. Finally, the concluding chapter addresses the implementation of learning to learn in the accounting curriculum, problems to consider in implementing change, and some suggestions for using intentional learning in accounting practice. (Francis et al. 1995, xi)

The monograph defines learning to learn as "a process of acquiring, understanding, and using a variety of strategies to improve one's ability to attain and apply knowledge, a process which results from, leads to, and enhances a questioning spirit and a lifelong desire to learn" (Francis et al. 1995, 6). It helps faculty understand some of the characteristics that affect student learning and how they can use teaching strategies to help students become intentional learners. It is an excellent tool for those faculty who truly want to help students break away from the mold of simply acquiring knowledge and begin the development of a process of learning to serve throughout their lifetimes.

International Exposure

The AECC was intended to focus on accounting education change in the United States. However, its impact had more far-reaching effects. The first international exposure came by chance. Gary Sundem had been named the AAA International Lecturer before accepting the position of Executive Director of the Commission. By the time he made his trip to Japan, Indonesia, Australia, and New Zealand in the fall of 1990, word about the Commission had spread. Most of his presentations were based on AECC activities. Although accounting education systems in each country were different, each with its own strengths and weaknesses, some elements of the AECC changes seemed to apply to each one.

The Commission made no attempt to publicize its activities outside the United States. Nevertheless, requests came for articles and presentations. The AECC was represented on the programs of the annual meetings of the European Accounting Association, the Irish Accounting and Finance Association, the Japan Accounting Association, the Canadian Academic Accounting Association, and the Academic Accounting Association of Australia and New Zealand, as well as at other international conferences. Requests for publications came from Great Britain (Sundem and Williams 1992), Germany (Williams and Sundem 1992), Ireland (Sundem 1995), and Canada (Sundem 1994).

Another fortuitous circumstance allowed further international exposure. In October 1992, the World Congress of Accountants and the accompanying International Accounting Education Conference were held in Washington D.C. Doyle Williams made a presentation on the work of the AECC at the Conference. Further, in connection with the Conference, Gary Sundem arranged for a tour of four grant schools (Brigham Young University, Arizona State University, University of Chicago, and University of Virginia) and the University of Southern California for 21 international delegates. The participants paid for the tour, and the consensus was that the insights gained were well worth the fee.

The United States may be leading the way for today's changes in accounting education, but it is clear that similar forces are fueling change around the globe. For example, Mueller (1995, 5) cites an Australian task force that was set up to explore how to "free up accounting programs to permit the inclusion of a broader range of subjects while maintaining the minimum level of skills felt necessary for professional accountants." Like the AECC, the Australian task force had representatives of the profession (the Institute of Chartered Accountants and the Society of CPAs) and academe (the Academic Accounting Association of Australia and New Zealand). The task force included an indirect reference to the AECC when it stated that "changes in accounting education are already underway in other parts of the world and the task force plans to investigate the suggested changes in these other countries before coming to its own recommended accreditation guidelines" (Mueller 1995, 5). A study for CGA Canada (Boyd 1995, 20) also referenced the AECC-recommended changes: "In our focus groups, CGA students, members and employers have described the role of the modern accountant as being similar to the model identified in the AECC materials."

Other international organizations sponsoring conferences on accounting education change include the International Federation of Accountants, the International Association for Accounting Education and Research, and the United Nations Intergovernmental Working Group of Financial Accounting and Reporting (which invited Doyle Williams to address its members on the work of the AECC). The AECC was certainly not the only impetus for such programs, but it has had a strong influence. Thus, the Commission has helped to pave the way and provide direction for accounting education change throughout the world.

Chapter 6
Position and Issues Statements

In addition to promoting change and implementing and monitoring the grant program, the Memorandum of Understanding establishing the AECC included the following:

> The Commission shall act as a forum for the identification, examination, and discussion of issues related to the education of accountants. The commission shall seek to identify the interests, concerns, and priorities of the most relevant stakeholders regarding the education of accountants and prospective changes thereto. *The Commission shall act as a catalyst for the cultivation of consensus* and promotion of actions among the various stakeholders in the reengineering of the education of accountants. (AECC 1989a, 5) [emphasis added]

To "act as a catalyst for the cultivation of consensus" the Commission needed a mechanism for preparing and exposing drafts of positions of the Commission. It was not sufficient to merely present the various sides of issues. The Commission had to try to forge a consensus and make that consensus known. To do this, it introduced two types of documents, Position Statements and Issues Statements. The two Position Statements and the six Issues Statements of the Commission are published in a single monograph (Accounting Education Change Commission and American Accounting Association 1996).

Position Statements, the more formal of the two document types, were conceived first. They required two votes of the Commission. A draft of a Position Statement would be authorized for exposure to the public by a 60 percent favorable vote of the Commission. Statements so authorized were to be widely disseminated for public comment. After making revisions based on the comments received, another 60 percent favorable vote was required for the Statement to become the official position of the Commission.

In August 1990 the Commission decided that timeliness of a Statement was more important than the exposure process. Thus was born the Issues Statement. Issues Statement No. 1, *AECC Urges Priority for Teaching in Higher Education*, was presented to the Commission, revised, and approved at that single meeting. With the benefit of hindsight, I believe the quick approval of this Statement was a mistake. It led to misunderstandings that could have been avoided by a proper exposure and revision process. While the other five Issues Statements were not as controversial, none of the six needed quick approval and could have gone through the exposure process of Position Statements. In fact, at least one did go through an exposure process and therefore could have been issued as a Position Statement.

Position Statement Number One

One of the major roadblocks to change in accounting education in the 1980s was lack of agreement on the directions of change. Even as the AECC began its efforts, such agreement was elusive. Barefield (1991, 307) summarized it as follows:

> I would argue that the RFP statement presumes too much agreement on the type of change required and, as noted earlier, that proponents of change err in believing that those 30 plus years of debate and the limited actions to date are viewed similarly by all concerned. There is great consensus that

change is needed but there is less agreement that the AECC and any or all of those other forces seeking change have a monopoly on an understanding of what types of change are appropriate or how they are to be achieved.

The Commission recognized this disagreement. But such disagreements are what had put accounting academe behind practice in reacting to a changing environment. Agreement on at least a general direction for change was necessary if the Commission was to carry out its task of fostering implementation of change rather than simply studying impacts of various changes.

The Commission was given an explicit mandate to implement the Bedford Committee report and Big 8 White Paper. It neither took this mandate lightly nor blindly accepted it. Much time during the Commission's first three meetings was spent developing its own interpretation of the direction of change. The timeline on preparation of Position Statement No. One, *Objectives of Education for Accountants*, was as follows:

- December 14, 1989—Draft of the Statement presented to the AECC by the Objectives of Education for Accountants Task Force (Jim Loebbecke and Gary Sundem)
- February 26, 1990—Commission approved the Statement for exposure after adding an appendix on "Learning to Learn"
- June 6, 1990—Commission discussed feedback received during the exposure period and asked the Executive Director to prepare a draft incorporating both public and Commission comments
- August 7, 1990—Position Statement No. One approved by a 13–1 vote

Position Statement No. One is by far the most often referenced Statement of the Commission. More than 17,000 copies were distributed. It broke no new ground, but it consolidated what the Commission members considered the most important parts of the Bedford Committee report and the Big 8 White Paper. The Statement first lists the desired capabilities in accounting graduates and then presents the implications of this for course and curriculum development and for instructional methods.

The first sentence under the heading "Desired Capabilities" sets the tone for the Statement: "Accounting programs should prepare students to **become** professional accountants, not to **be** professional accountants at the time of entry to the profession" [bold in the original]. The Statement focuses on accounting education, not accounting training, although it does not use those words. It sees undergraduate accounting education as the building of a base upon which specialized knowledge and training can be built.

The most controversial part of the Statement, as reflected in the public comments received, is that "[s]pecialized accounting education…should be offered primarily at the post-baccalaureate level and via continuing education." The Commission did not regard this as an endorsement of five-year programs for entry to the profession. In contrast, the common background for all entering the profession should be a broad, conceptual understanding of accounting and its role in economic decisions. I think a majority of the Commission members believed that specialized education is necessary for success in the accounting profession. However, it is not needed at the time of entry, and it can be achieved by a variety of methods, only one of which is graduate accounting education.

Another controversial interpretation of the Statement was the emphasis on liberal arts education. Barefield (1991, 310–311), among others, criticized the view that additional liberal arts education would enhance students' ability to think critically and to communicate well. Although Position Statement No. One did not explicitly recommend an increase in the liberal arts component of accounting education, much of the discussion surrounding the Statement did. However, the Commission's recommendation was the *integration* of liberal arts and professional education, not simply the addition of more liberal arts courses.

Commission member Joan Stark, in her monograph *Strengthening the Ties that Bind* (Stark and Lowther 1988), criticizes the "separate but equal" view of liberal arts and professional education present on many campuses. She rejects "timeframe tinkering," that is, using distribution requirements to increase the liberal arts component of professional education. In his introduction to the monograph, former President of Cornell University Frank Rhodes stated: "Too many institutions have simply added more liberal arts courses to already burdensome programs of professional education. Rarely have they attempted to integrate liberal and professional education in ways that have meaning for all students; rarely have they been able to link high standards of scholarship and professional practice to critical thinking on the fundamental issues of life" (Stark and Lowther 1988, 1).

Everyone agrees that graduates should be able to think critically, relate to others, make ethical judgments, and communicate. Too often both liberal arts and professional faculties consider these areas to be the domain of the liberal arts. Professional faculties criticize the liberal arts for not doing them well, and liberal arts faculties decry their lack of time to accomplish them. This conflict, in addition to battles over students and resources, has led to a separation between liberal arts and professional education and educators. The solution is not more or less coursework in either area, but the integration of the liberal arts values into the professional curriculum.

Responding to the AECC's emphasis on liberal arts values by a simple increase in the number of "arts, humanities, and sciences" courses would be counterproductive. In many universities, such a requirement could (and probably would) be satisfied by courses that did not accomplish the desired objectives. Thus, an accounting program that met the AECC's objective by simply requiring additional liberal arts courses would probably harm rather than improve the program. Students would view the courses as a necessary evil, and the values would not be carried over into their accounting and business classes.

If the position of the Commission had been made more clearly, programs would have placed more emphasis on using techniques from good liberal arts programs to enhance the accounting curriculum's ability to teach students to think, relate, and communicate. More of a liberal arts approach to the accounting curriculum could also instill in students a greater appreciation for accounting's role in and contributions to society. The answer is not additional liberal arts courses but making accounting and business courses more like good liberal arts courses.

Teaching introductory accounting as a liberal arts topic is not a new idea. Courtney Brown (1964), then Dean of the Columbia Graduate School of Business, suggested:

> Any subject that is taught in the great liberating tradition of teaching can be made a liberal art. This tradition minimizes the descriptive and instead it emphasizes the perspective of historical development, the analytical significance of the material to other important aspects of society, and its comparative characteristics and values in differing cultures. This sounds like we must be getting pretty far away from the first course in accounting and I suspect we will, as the first accounting course is now taught.

He went on to suggest that to attract students with the intelligence and other traits required in accounting, the introductory accounting course, like a course in Chaucer, must be taught in the liberal tradition. The AECC did not need to break new ground; it just needed to repeat this plea of nearly 30 years ago.

Appendix A of Position Statement No. One, "Learning to Learn," has also received much attention. It states that "programs focused on teaching students how to learn must address three issues: (1) content, (2) process, and (3) attitudes." However, the Statement did not give much guidance on how to accomplish this. Therefore, the Commission devoted additional attention to this issue and five years later produced a monograph elaborating on the concept (Francis et al. 1995). This monograph was discussed in more detail in chapter 5 of this monograph.

Position Statement Number Two

On November 8, 1990, the Student Recruiting Task Force (later known as the Student Quality Task Force) proposed development of a Statement on the introductory accounting course. The

Chair of the Task force, Rick Elam, led the development of a draft Statement, which was presented to the Commission on January 17, 1991. After several iterations, and with the considerable help of Bob Elliott and Joan Stark, the Commission approved exposure of the Statement on February 11, 1992. On May 14, 1992, the Commission revised the Statement based on comments received and unanimously approved the final Statement, which was titled "The First Course in Accounting."

It is significant that the Student Recruiting (Quality) Task Force was charged with developing this Statement. The Commission clearly believed that this course is a major factor in determining who enters accounting programs and who doesn't. Although only the following brief section deals directly with this issue, the entire Statement is consistent with the goal of attracting the best and brightest to accounting:

> The first course has even more significance for those considering a career in accounting and those otherwise open to the option of majoring in accounting. The course shapes their perceptions of (1) the profession, (2) the aptitudes and skills needed for successful careers in accounting, and (3) the nature of career opportunities in accounting. These perceptions affect whether the supply of talent will be sufficient for the profession to thrive.

The Commission spent much time discussing how to attract the best students to accounting. However, other than this Statement and work at Kansas State University as part of its AECC grant, the Commission did little to directly influence the ways accounting programs attract students. The problem was evident in a 1991 study by the AICPA (AICPA and Gallup Organization 1991). The study found that both high school and college students ranked accounting last among the six top professions; medicine, law, teaching, engineering, and financial planning were all ranked as substantially more desirable than accounting. The most common task they attributed to accountants was preparing tax returns. They perceived that being an accountant requires honesty, problem-solving ability, and a numerical orientation. The college students had an especially unfavorable view of accountants, with only about one-third responding that accounting requires working with people and nearly one-half responding that it is boring. It is from a population with this attitude that accounting programs are trying to attract the best and the brightest. This is a formidable task.

The major theme of Position Statement No. Two is summarized as follows: "In general, the first course in accounting should be an *introduction to accounting* rather than *introductory accounting*" (emphasis in the original). Although the Statement includes both the preparation and use of accounting information as appropriate for the first course, the details of the Statement clearly favor an emphasis on the use of information.

Students in the first course in accounting should "learn about accounting as an information development and communication function that supports economic decision-making." The approach advocated is almost a liberal-arts approach to accounting, where students learn *about* accounting not how to *do* accounting. Teaching methods should focus on student involvement and discovery, not knowledge transfer.

The introductory accounting course had been criticized for many years before the AECC issued its Statement. In the early 1970s, the Price Waterhouse Foundation sponsored a study group (see Mueller 1971) that recommended many of the same things that appear in the AECC Statement. At a conference in 1973, Bill Gifford (1973, 12), a partner at Price Waterhouse and Secretary of the Foundation, said: "Educators and practitioners have been saying for years that the Introductory Accounting Course should be changed....It seems to me that a change is needed and needed now....With a truly challenging introductory course for undergraduates, a good student would begin to appreciate that a knowledge of accounting and its significance is today just as much an essential part of the cultivated and educated mind as are other subjects that have been generally accorded this status."

Thus, the AECC did not initiate a movement toward user-oriented first courses in accounting. It jumped on a bandwagon that had already gained much momentum. Nevertheless, by emphasizing the importance of the first course and advocating that it be taught by "the most effective instructors," the Commission added to the momentum.

The themes of this Statement were taken a step farther in a study sponsored and published by the California Society of CPAs (1995). Led by Paul Solomon, the California Society's Committee on Accounting Education set out to help faculty "implement the changes recommended in the AECC's Position Statement Number Two entitled *The First Course in Accounting*" (California Society of CPAs 1995, 3). The Committee developed the "California Core Competency Model," a listing of the outcomes and core competencies to be generated by the first course in accounting. A total of 12 competencies are defined in three general areas:

Financial Accounting
    1) Accounting's Role in Society
    2) Fundamental Business Concepts
    3) Fundamental Accounting Concepts Underlying Financial Statements
    4) Uses and Limitations of Financial Statements
    5) Accounting Information Systems
Managerial Accounting
    6) Role of the Management Accountant
    7) Using Accounting Information to Make Decisions
    8) Using Accounting Information to Analyze and Improve Operational Efficiency
    9) Processing Managerial Accounting Information
Active Learning
    10) Communication Skills
    11) Group Work Skills
    12) Problem-Solving Skills

This model is an excellent supplement to the AECC's Position Statement.

Issues Statement Number 1

August 7, 1990, was an important day for the Commission. On that day it approved what was arguably its most important and certainly its most controversial Statement, *AECC Urges Priority for Teaching in Higher Education*. It was originally approved as a press release. However, to give it more permanence, it was later called an Issues Statement. Unlike Position Statements, the newly created category of Issues Statements did not require exposure before issuance.

As I mentioned in the introduction to this chapter, I think avoiding exposure and thereby not considering comments of others before issuing this Statement was a mistake. Many Commission members would probably disagree. The controversy it created was not all bad. However, both supporters and opponents of the Statement misinterpreted parts of it, and such misinterpretations might have been avoided by more careful wording based on initial reactions to an exposure of the Statement.

The Commission was seeking rather than avoiding controversy with this Statement: "Giving teaching and curriculum and course development a more important role will require major changes in the recruitment, development, and evaluation of faculty members. The Commission is aware that these changes will be controversial." It was meant to challenge the status quo. But it was not meant to be so extreme as to alienate a part of the academic community that would have an influential role in the future of accounting education. Unfortunately, such alienation did occur.

The main problem was that a segment of the accounting research community interpreted the Statement as "research bashing." They believed that elevating the stature of teaching necessarily lowered the stature of research. In our limited-resource world, they were probably right. However, the Commission was careful to not rank research and teaching priorities. The majority of the Commission clearly believed that research and other scholarly activities are important—probably more important than ever because of the accelerating rate of change. But they also believed that teaching and course and curriculum development were not emphasized enough in university performance evaluation and reward systems.

I do not think the Commission intended to bash research, but it was willing to accept a reduction in the emphasis placed on research in order to increase the attention to teaching-related issues. There needs to be a balance between teaching and research, one that recognizes the synergy between the two. The Commission believed that the balance had been lost and needed to be restored. Some opponents of the Statement felt that its goal was to do more than redress the balance, that its objective was to make teaching activities dominate research activities in our colleges and universities. Their concern was legitimate, and there were members of the Commission as well as others who shared the concern.

This concern was not helped by the interpretation of the Statement by some supporters. They were happy to interpret the Statement as research bashing. In fact, they championed exactly the position that the research community feared—that teaching should dominate accounting academe. Unlike the Commission, their goal was not restoring balance but swinging the pendulum to the opposite extreme.

The controversy created by this Statement had the positive effect of increasing the visibility of the debate over change in accounting education. It brought into the open issues that had been simmering for some time. But there were also negative effects, the largest of which was losing the support of some important members of the academic community. Could this have been avoided? Maybe.

One segment of the Commission favored a stronger, and therefore a more controversial, Statement, one that placed the priority of teaching above that of research. The initial draft had language about the relationship of research and teaching that would have alienated the research community much more than did the final Statement. One of the reasons advocates favored a stronger Statement was that they believed the current system was so entrenched that only an extreme position on the opposite side would cause any movement at all.

Another segment of the Commission was sensitive to reactions in the research community. Although they agreed that more emphasis on teaching and course and curriculum development was warranted, they didn't want the pendulum to swing back too far.

As a result of these opposing views, the Commission intentionally avoided addressing the relative roles of research and teaching in the accounting academy, and it was this avoidance that created ambiguity and the potential for misinterpretations about its position. It would not have been possible to get unanimity on the Commission regarding the relationship, and it might have caused a split on the Commission that would have negatively affected its other activities. Nevertheless, with hindsight I think it would have been good to try to agree on a position. A well-reasoned compromise position, neither bashing nor exulting either research or teaching, might have at least avoided the ambiguity. But it also might have been such a neutral Statement that it would have gone relatively unnoticed and had little impact.

A possible compromise position is one eloquently presented by Beaver (1992). He regrets the fact that many in both academe and practice seem to view research and teaching as competitors rather then complements. To him the real issue is the nature of accounting research, not the balance of teaching and research. Both teaching and research require a blend of theory, empirical research, and knowledge of accounting institutions. The proper blend will allow both teaching and research to prosper. A well-reasoned position such as Beaver's might not have received the attention afforded Issues Statement No. 1, but it might have served as a better base for building changes in accounting educational programs.

The other controversial area of the Statement was the invitation for outside parties to exert their influence on accounting education. Especially troublesome was the invitation to legislatures and governors to become involved. The wording sounded innocuous, asking them to "endorse effective teaching and curriculum and course development as priorities." This is essentially an open invitation for them to become involved in internal resource allocations in colleges and universities. I have to agree with the critics of this part of the Statement. Legislators and governors have political motives for interfering in university resource allocations, and even if their intervention might help accounting education in this instance, I believe the long-run effects of such interventions would be detrimental. Not only do they have potential political motives, they also lack knowledge of the trade-offs made in such resource allocation decisions.

Although the Statement had its critics, it also had its supporters. The AECC sought endorsement of the Statement from a variety of organizations. Among those endorsing the Statement were the Executive Committee of the American Accounting Association, the American Institute of Certified Public Accountants, Beta Alpha Psi, the Financial Executives Institute, the Federation of Schools of Accountancy, the Institute of Management Accountants, the California Society of Certified Public Accountants, the Colorado Society of Certified Public Accountants, the Illinois Society of Certified Public Accountants, the New York State Society of Certified Public Accountants, and the Texas Society of Certified Public Accountants.

In summary, the Statement accomplished most of what it was intended to achieve. If no one had been upset by it, the Statement probably would have been less effective in focusing attention on an important issue, one that has no easy solution but one that is essential to the future of accounting education.

Issues Statement Number 2

In its early meetings, the Commission spent much time discussing the effect of the CPA examination on the quality of accounting education. The consensus seemed to be that the examination, as currently structured, impeded progress. Much of the educational focus on rules and regulations was derived from a desire to prepare students for the CPA examination. In the end, the only Statement the Commission made regarding the examination was Issues Statement No. 2, *AECC Urges Decoupling of Academic Studies and Professional Accounting Examination Preparation*.

This Statement was as significant for what it did not contain as for its actual content. The Commission discussed several issues on which it elected to not comment. Discussions of one issue, the content of the CPA examination, extended the entire life of the AECC, with progress behind the scenes but with no formal Statement being prepared.

The Professional Examinations Task Force was one of the more active task forces throughout the life of the Commission. Shortly after the task forces were formed, the Regulatory Issues Task Force was merged into Professional Examinations because their agendas had nearly 100 percent overlap. Nathan Garrett, Sarah Blake, and Rick Elam were the primary AECC players in this task force. The task force's first report, on June 6, 1990, laid out the following issues:

- Meeting educational requirement before being allowed to sit for professional examinations
- Release of pass rates by school on the CPA examination
- Secure examinations (no release of past questions and answers)
- Requirement for 150 semester hours of postsecondary education to sit for the CPA examination
- National (vs. state) requirements for certification
- How to assess communication skills on the CPA examination
- Content of the CPA examination

Although the task force had the title "Professional Examinations," it is clear from this set of issues that the initial focus was the CPA examination. While it is true that Issues Statement No. 2 was broader than the CPA examination, the Commission's continuing attention remained focused on the CPA examination with only passing reference to the CMA and CIA examinations. While some might interpret this as an unwarranted focus on public accounting, I think it was an appropriate focus. The Commission was not interested in the examinations *per se* but on their influence on accounting education. The CPA examination has certainly had a major influence on the accounting curriculum and on other aspects of accounting programs; the CMA and CIA examinations have not.

When it presented these issues, the task force recommended against pursuing two of them, national requirements for certification and assessing communication skills on the CPA examination, and the Commission agreed. The Commission also reiterated a decision it implicitly made at its first meeting—to not address the 150-hour requirement. Later the Commission decided to not pursue the issues of pass rates on the CPA examination and secure examinations. Except for the 150-hour requirement and possibly the assessment of communication skills on the CPA examination, these issues were deemed to have little effect on accounting education.

Before the Commission decided to not take a position on the publication of pass rates on the CPA examination, its discussions led to criticisms of an anticipated position opposing such publication. The Big 8 White Paper stated that "passing the CPA examination should not be the goal of accounting education." Although I believe most Commission members wholeheartedly agreed with that Statement, they were not willing to exclude professional examination pass rates as one possible outcome measure for certain types of programs. Preparing students to pass a certification examination was not a sufficient measure of an accounting program, although combined with other measures it might provide useful information about a program. The Commission agreed with its critics that a program that did not give graduates the skills and knowledge to become professionally certified was probably deficient, as was one that gave them only the skills and knowledge to pass the examination and nothing more.

Another issue that received discussion in early Commission meetings, but which was not addressed by the task force, was examination timing. There was some sentiment to try to change the examination's frequency to once a year and to have the examination offered in late summer. This proposal never went beyond the discussion stage.

On August 7, 1990, the Commission took its first official action related to professional examinations, approving the following resolution: "The AECC recommends that candidates who wish to sit for professional examinations be required to complete all educational requirements before applying to sit for the examination." This was later broadened into Issues Statement No. 2, which was approved the following June. Subsequently, the Statement was endorsed by the Council of the AICPA and was included in the proposed Uniform Accountancy Act.

The title of Issues Statement No. 2 is slightly misleading. The word "decoupling" is stronger than the language in the body of the Statement. Only two points are made in the Statement: (1) students should not be allowed to sit for a professional certification examination, be it CPA, CMA, or CIA, before they have completed the education required for certification, and (2) courses designed primarily to provide review for professional examinations should not be given academic credit. By decoupling academic studies and examination preparation, the Commission did not mean to imply that academic studies should not prepare students for the examinations. It simply meant that there should be more to academic studies than examination preparation, and by focusing on reviewing for a professional examination before completing one's academic studies, students do not receive the full benefit of the academic studies.

This Statement could have been seen as a way to avoid the difficult issue of the content of the CPA examination. Those looking only at the published Statements of the Commission could easily draw that conclusion. However, rather than avoiding the issue, I believe the Commission simply admitted that examination changes have a very long time-horizon, and a short-term expedient should be implemented even while trying to influence the long-term content of the examination.

Working primarily through the AICPA and the National Association of State Boards of Accountancy (NASBA), the Commission began a dialog on the CPA examination contents. LaVern Johnson, Chairman of the AICPA Board of Examiners, became a member of the task force in early 1993, and meetings were held with the AICPA staff responsible for the Uniform CPA Examination. At the same time the task force developed an Exposure Draft, "Proposed Content Specifications for the Uniform CPA Examination." In August 1993, in the interests of early submission, this Exposure Draft was turned into a letter to the AICPA Board of Examiners. The goal was to increase the examination's focus on testing higher-order learning skills. In a report back to the Commission in April 1995, Rick Elam reported that the AECC had been influential in moving the Board of Examiners and its preparation subcommittees to directly consider cognitive skill level in preparing the examinations.

In 1994, an additional issue relating to the CPA examination arose: how State Boards review transcripts of candidates from nontraditional programs. This issue arose because the Brigham Young University program, among others, did not have courses with the typical titles required in some state regulations. BYU graduates were being denied the opportunity to sit for the CPA examination because they had not taken the "appropriate courses." The AECC wanted regulations changed so that they required specific course content, not specific course titles. Then, in October 1993, the AICPA and NASBA proposed Uniform Accountancy Act rules that threatened to make matters worse. The rules listed total credit hours and course titles that must appear on a potential candidate's transcript before he or she may sit for the CPA examination. In a letter to the Board of Examiners, the Commission urged the AICPA and NASBA to revise the model rules to avoid this problem.

The ongoing nature of the CPA examination issues was confirmed when, at the very last AECC meeting, the Professional Examinations Task Force was still seeking Commission input. The task force was preparing a draft letter and questionnaire response to the AICPA Board of Examiners on computerization of the examination and the testing of higher order cognitive skills.

Issues Statements Numbers 3 and 6

Two Issues Statements related to two-year colleges: Issues Statement No. 3, *The Importance of Two-Year Colleges for Accounting Education*; and Issues Statement No. Six, *Transfer of Academic Credit for the First Course in Accounting Between Two-Year and Four-Year Colleges*. The topic of two-year colleges first arose during the Commission's early discussions of the grant program. Concern was expressed that the grants did nothing to motivate changes at two-year colleges.

The AECC's charge did not mention two-year colleges, and no two-year college representative was placed on the Commission. Some Commission members and top officials of the sponsoring firms expressed the opinion that two-year college education was not part of the "professional" education of accountants. Other Commission members were convinced that the two-year colleges played an important role in professional accounting education and that their participation in change activities was essential for the widespread introduction of desired changes.

It took a year for the Commission to really commit to exploring the role of two-year colleges in accounting education and how they might affect the change process. The Two-Year College Task Force met for the first time in July 1990. It spent the next year gathering information and making the case for the importance of two-year colleges in the change process. The Commission's education about two-year colleges culminated with a presentation in August 1991 by Dennis Greer, Tom Hilgerman, and Lynn Mazzola, all two-year college faculty and members of the task force. I believe that even the skeptical Commission members became convinced that ignoring two-year colleges in the change process invited failure. By the end of 1991 the Commission had committed $100,000 to a special grant program for two-year colleges (as described in chapter 4), but that alone did not seem adequate.

As Issues Statement No. 3 points out, more than half of the national enrollment in the first course in accounting is at two-year colleges, and about one-fourth of those entering the accounting profession took their initial accounting coursework at a two-year college. A survey taken by the Commission during 1991–92 found that 19 percent of those joining the AICPA in the last ten years and 27 percent of the members of the Institute of Management Accountants took their first accounting course at a two-year college. Administrators of four-year accounting programs indicated that the percentage of their graduates who took their initial accounting courses at two-year colleges had increased in the past five years and was expected to continue increasing. These survey results confirm that two-year colleges play a significant and increasing role in introducing students to accounting.

If change does not occur at two-year colleges, two major negative impacts arise. First, accounting programs will fail to attract many of the best and the brightest, those on whom the future of the profession rests. Second, a large number of those entering the accounting profession will have an education built on a shaky base. Therefore, the Commission was convinced that two-year colleges needed to be involved in the program changes.

Many accounting educators and professionals continued to view two-year colleges in the role many played in the 1970s, as primarily remedial institutions for students who did not have the qualifications for the four-year school. To convince them of the growing importance of two-year colleges, the Commission prepared Issues Statement No. 3 and released it in August 1992. Based on the Commission's conclusion that "the quality of education provided by two-year colleges has an important effect on the overall quality of accounting education," it encouraged cooperation between administrators of two-year and four-year accounting programs. Sharing information and cooperating in curriculum change activities "can enhance the quality of both two-year and four-year programs." The concluding paragraph of the Statement reiterated that the "Commission believes that the involvement of two-year colleges in accounting education change is critical for improving the overall quality of accounting education."

Issues Statement No. 3 extolled the virtues of cooperation between two-year and four-year schools, but it provided little guidance beyond the general sharing of information. At an open forum at the 1992 AAA Annual Meeting, one of the major issues raised was the transfer of credit from two-year to four-year schools. This topic continued to simmer until an *ad hoc* Articulation Task Force was appointed in October 1993. (The Two-Year College Task Force was eliminated in the task-force restructuring at the beginning of the 1992–93 year.) Within the next year, and with the help of non-Commission members Linda Lessing, Paul Solomon, and Mary Tharp, the Task force prepared a draft Statement. The Commission presented the proposed Statement to the February 1995 AECC workshop on the first course in accounting for feedback before formally issuing it. After incorporating the feedback, in April 1995 the Commission approved for publication Issues Statement No. 6, *Transfer of Academic Credit for the First Course in Accounting Between Two-Year and Four-Year Colleges*.

Although the initial intent was to address the issue of transfers from a two-year school using a traditional curriculum to a four-year school using a revised curriculum, it soon became evident that the opposite was also occurring. Several two-year schools were at or near the forefront of change activities, especially pedagogical changes such as increased emphasis on communication and interpersonal skills and the incorporation of technology in the curriculum. The articulation problem became one of transfer from one school to another with a significantly different curriculum, whatever the differences.

The body of the Statement does a good job of framing the issue, but the greatest help to schools will come from the two appendices. The Statement says that "renegotiating transferability agreements to focus on skills and knowledge (sometimes called student outcomes) and activities intended to develop the agreed-upon set of skills and knowledge is one approach to assuring transfer of academic credit for the introductory accounting sequence in the face of episodic or continual curriculum change." Appendix A of the Statement, "Student Competencies as a Basis of Transferability Agreements," shows one way to do this. Appendix B, "Suggestions for Two-Year College Faculty Who Wish to Redesign the Introductory Accounting Sequence," gives advice on how two-year faculty might want to consider articulation agreements when revising their curriculum.

Appendix A is derived largely from *The California Core Competency Model for the First Course in Accounting* (California Society of CPAs 1995). That document indicated that "Paul Solomon of San Jose State University led the effort to improve articulation, develop the competencies, and secure their adoption" (California Society of CPAs 1995, 1). Paul also contributed greatly to Issues Statement No. 6. The key to appendix A is measuring transferable skills and knowledge, not transferable courses. Accounting curricula build on the skills and knowledge students have gained in previous courses. When preceding courses are nearly identical, regardless of where they were taken, transfer requirements based on courses are appropriate. But when changes occur in the curriculum, it is necessary to resort to assuring that transfer students have the requisite knowledge and skills, not just a prescribed set of courses.

Appendix B of the Statement provides help to two-year schools that want to revise their accounting program but fear a negative effect on transferability. In the past, the attitude at many four-year schools was that the two-year schools should "follow our lead." But recently it is not always clear that the four-year school is in the lead, and there may be different types of changes in the different four-year schools to which two-year graduates transfer. There is no foolproof way to deal with such complex situations, but Appendix B presents a process that worked for at least one two-year college.

Issues Statement Number 4
One of the major obstacles to change encountered by the Commission was a faculty belief that recruiters look for technical competence in graduates, not breadth and adaptability. In other words, the changes advocated may be appropriate for long-term career success, but they are contrary to what will lead to short-term success in finding a job after graduation. Burton and Sack (1991, 122) summarized this position:

> [W]e had the uncomfortable feeling that the local office field recruiter did not share the vision of their Managing Partners. We can understand why they might be a little hesitant. It is one thing to ask that the firm's future partners, hired from the local university, have judgment and perspective and a commitment to continued education. It is quite another thing to put those high-minded people to work as soon as they come on board, billing them out at $30 an hour for at least 2,000 hours in their first year.

In addition, the broader skills and knowledge advocated by the Commission were not often employed in the first year or two of work. This was especially true in jobs in public accounting. It placed students from programs that implement AECC-endorsed changes at a disadvantage compared to those from programs that focused on specific job applications encountered during the first year or two of work. Such a view was the opposite of the theme of the Big 8 White Paper. Nevertheless, the prevailing view was that the heads of major accounting firms may believe the White Paper, but their recruiters and first-level supervisors did not.

This view led to the formation of the Early Employment Experience (E^3) Task Force. It was asked to explore the "interfacing of the education of the 'new' accountant with the initial employment experience." Burton and Sack (1991, 122) placed a great burden on this task force: "The AECC was wise to have established a task force to look at the early employment experience of recruits. In our judgment, the work of that task force will be critical to the ultimate success of the work of the entire commission." The task force focused on the "gap" between student expectations and the realities of the work environment. The task force was also to give consideration to "recruiting signaling on campuses," but it devoted less attention to this issue.

Before the E^3 Task Force developed its program, the Commission did two things to address the issue of recruiter signaling on campus. First, it prepared a list of "dos and don'ts" for recruiters of accounting students. Second, either Doyle Williams or Gary Sundem made presentations to the recruiting partners of all Big 6 accounting firms.

The E^3 Task Force had three main accomplishments. First, the main themes were published in an article in *Accounting Horizons* (Elliott 1991). Although this article did not have the official endorsement of the Commission, it effectively presented the concerns being addressed by the AECC. It addressed both short-term and long-term improvement opportunities. Among the short-term items were:

- Recruiting—Create more long-term incentives for recruiters, such as rewarding them based on how many of their recruits make partner (or at least make greater than normal progress toward promotion).
- Transition from education to practice—Make the transition more gradual through increased use of internships and work-study or cooperative education programs.
- Continuing professional education—Incorporate technical content that is removed from academic programs into the CPE programs of employees.
- Job assignments—Provide more choice in job assignment and more challenging assignments.
- Personnel management—Tie performance evaluations to traits associated with career success rather than successful completion of narrow tasks, and increase the use of mentoring.
- Job image—Recruiters should articulate the "social, economic, and professional value of accountancy's products."

Long-term suggestions centered on creating opportunities for staff by creating more value for clients. Employers should treat people as human capital that is to be developed and protected. They should make each employee an important part of a knowledge network that provides information support to decision makers.

Second, the task force worked internally within the largest public accounting firms to change both recruiting practices and the deployment and evaluation of entry-level staff. While there is no documented evidence of the success of this effort, I think most faculty would agree that there was a noticeable difference in recruiting emphases and some progress in first- and second-year experiences of staff accountants over the decade of the 1990s. Today, most recruiters routinely seek the kind of breadth and conceptual understanding advocated by the Commission, whether the recruiters are from large international public accounting firms, local and regional firms, or industry.

Finally, Issues Statement No. 4, *Improving the Early Employment Experience of Accountants*, was approved in March 1993. With the help of non-Commission members James Deitrick (University of Texas at Austin), Brian Jemelian (Price Waterhouse), and Jean Wyer (Coopers & Lybrand), the task force prepared recommendations for the following: (1) faculty members, (2) students, (3) career planning and placement professionals, (4) recruiters, (5) supervisors of early work experience, (6) workplace educators of first- through third-year employees, and (7) employer management. The appendix gave suggestions about how each of the recommendations could be accomplished. More than any other Commission document, this was a "how to" book on methods for accomplishing the Commission's objectives.

Casual observation indicates that the easy items, especially those relating to recruiting, are being reasonably well addressed. The jury is still out on the more difficult changes, both those in academe and those in practice. Elliott (1991, 119) called the task force "a first approximation of an Accounting Practice Change Commission." Although accounting practice is undergoing many changes, attention to the early employment experiences of staff is not the top priority. However slow, progress is being made.

Issues Statement Number 5

Issues Statement No. 5, *Evaluating and Rewarding Effective Teaching*, has the potential to be one of the AECC's most important Statements. However, because it was issued late in the Commission's life, it did not receive as much attention as earlier Statements. This Statement is a natural follow-up to Issues Statement No.1 that urged priority for teaching in higher education. However, this is a more positive document— not one that simply "urges" changes but one that provides help in guiding change.

It seems well accepted outside the academy (and even by many within the academy) that research is over-emphasized to the detriment of teaching in our colleges and universities. But few faculty or administrators in accounting programs would say that this has been an intentional goal of their schools or programs. Yes, research is important. Hardly anyone wants to go back to the situation of the 1950s where many accounting programs focused on merely teaching students how to do what accountants do. But research and teaching should have a synergy, where each improves the quality of the other. A research-oriented faculty should increase the intellectual development of accounting students. Researchers are probably not the best ones to provide training—learning of facts and techniques—but they should provide a more fertile environment for learning critical-thinking and problem-solving skills.

If teaching and research can be synergistic, why is the belief so widespread that a research emphasis reduces the quality of teaching? My hypothesis—and one that many academic colleagues agree with—is that the traditional academic incentive system motivates many faculty to shift enough effort from teaching to research to more than offset the beneficial synergies of the two. The switch is not because research is inherently more valued but because the measurement system used in most colleges and universities is biased toward research.

Why are measurement systems biased toward research? Because we have much more confidence in evaluations of research quality (based on peer review, publication, and wide exposure of research output) than in those of teaching quality (based primarily on student evaluations). Therefore, we are willing to reward (and punish) faculty based more on their research evaluations than on their teaching evaluations. In addition, research quality is widely known and accepted outside of one's own college or university, while teaching quality is generally an internal measure that is hard to compare across schools. Therefore, it is a potentially noisy signal to outsiders and therefore easily discounted.

What does all of this have to do with Issues Statement No. 5? If better measures of teaching performance could be developed, measures that include all aspects of teaching, the emphasis on teaching would naturally increase without any negative aspersions on the value of research. The Statement by itself falls short of providing the needed framework and measurement methods. But it is a start that can contribute to the necessary dialog.

The Statement includes five important characteristics of effective teaching (curriculum design and course development, use of well-conceived course materials, presentation skills, well-chosen pedagogical methods and assessment devices, and guidance and advising), but I think it ignores one essential characteristic: in-depth, up-to-date knowledge of the subject. The characteristics shown are all process oriented, but teaching in a professional program such as accounting takes more than process. If a faculty member's repertoire is limited to what is available in published materials, he or she can't bring to the classroom personal insights that are not readily available elsewhere, and students are being shortchanged. Both research and professional qualifications can add a needed dimension—each in its own way. A college or university's mission will determine the correct balance of research and professional expertise among the faculty. If the maintenance of this expertise is not measured and rewarded, the teaching program will suffer.

An especially helpful part of the Statement is a list of strategies for evaluating and improving teaching, including self assessment, observations by colleagues, student evaluations, alumni input,

instructional consultants, and teaching portfolios. None of these is developed enough in the Statement to give clear direction on how to apply them, but a good bibliography is included for those
interested in pursuing them further.

Summary

The Position and Issues Statements of the Commission are a permanent record of the most
important recommendations of the AECC. They are not perfect, but they provide important insights into topics that are essential to the change process in accounting. They are generally succinct
and readable. I recommend them to anyone interested in the lasting impact of the Commission.

Chapter 7
IMPACTS ON STAKEHOLDERS

The most important stakeholders to be influenced by the AECC are accounting faculty and administrators. Most of this monograph describes how the Commission tried to accomplish this. However, the ultimate success of the changes in accounting education also depends on how much support is generated among other stakeholders. This chapter addresses the impact of the Commission on the following stakeholders: (1) public accounting practitioners, including those in both large and small firms, (2) accounting practitioners in business, industry, and government, (3) business school and university administrators, and (4) accrediting agencies, especially the AACSB-The International Association For Management Education.

A generalization that summarizes the Commission's impact on all of these stakeholders is that progress was made with leadership groups, but there was much less impact at grass-roots levels. Presentations were made to the Boards of Directors of the AICPA and the Financial Executives Institute. Other interactions with organizations such as the Institute of Management Accountants and the Institute of Internal Auditors were primarily with staff and a few top leaders. These groups generally gave enthusiastic support to AECC initiatives, but most members of the organizations were oblivious to the existence of the Commission.

A December 1991 survey (Hulme and Ehrenreich 1994) pointed out the differences between educators and practitioners in their views on needed changes. Practitioners were randomly selected from AICPA and IMA rosters, so they were typical members, not necessarily leaders. In total, the practitioners felt less need to change than did the educators, although both groups strongly supported change. In addition, the practitioners wanted more emphasis on specialized courses, particularly tax, more coverage of procedures and standards, and more real-world cases and problems. Educators wanted a greater conceptual focus, more critical thinking, and more communication skills. The views of the educators were much more consistent with the wishes of the leadership of practitioner organizations than were those of the average practitioners. Either the message had not reached a majority of practitioners or they had heard the message but did not agree with it.

The Commission's lack of recognition among the majority of practicing accountants was not a critical impediment to achieving its objectives. Nevertheless, accounting programs implementing changes must be concerned if a majority of the practicing community are either not supportive of changes, or, worse, want changes in the opposite direction from those being implemented.

Next let's look at the impact of the Commission on the four practitioner groups mentioned earlier.

Public Accounting Practitioners—Large Firms

The AECC was created and funded by the then Big 8 public accounting firms, and it was answerable to the Sponsors' Task Force, which was composed of top personnel partners from the firms. The Commission Chairman and Executive Director met regularly with the Sponsors' Task Force and periodically with the Managing Partners of the firms. Two representatives of the large accounting firms were on the Commission. Indeed, the avowed purpose of the Commission was to carry out the directives in the White Paper prepared by these firms. Therefore, both awareness of and support for the Commission's activities at the top levels of the large public accounting firms was great.

In fact, the consonance of the AECC activities and the desires of the large accounting firms drew criticism. For example, Davis and Sherman (1994, 16) maintained that "the financial linkages between the Big Eight and the professoriate suggest control of the Bedford committee and the AECC by the Big Eight." Later, they state that "it appears that the AAA has been captured [by] the Big Eight accounting firms through the creation and operation of the AECC...[T]he initiatives of the Change Commission operate in such a way as to advance the purposes and interests of the Sponsoring Firms" (Davis and Sherman 1994, 20).

I don't think anyone connected with the AECC would suggest that the Commission did not try to advance the interests of the sponsoring firms. A primary measure of the success of the Commission is whether it sufficiently advanced these interests. The large accounting firms are major employers of accounting graduates, and to ignore their needs would be foolhardy. A more important question, though, is whether advancing the interests of the large accounting firms was at the expense of the interests of other stakeholders. I will address that issue later in this chapter.

There is little doubt that the large accounting firms exerted an influence on the AECC, but did the AECC also influence the firms? I think the answer is a qualified "yes." There were two areas in which influencing these firms was important to the success of the Commission. First, the hiring practices and the deployment of new graduates had to be consistent with the recommendations of the Commission. Second, the firms had a right (and probably an obligation) to make known the knowledge, skills, and abilities they wanted in accountants they hired out of accounting programs, but the Commission seemed to believe (without explicitly stating so) that it was up to the colleges and universities to determine the best way to develop these attributes in students.

Consider first the hiring practices of the large firms. In the Commission's early years, many academics voiced concern that the attributes delineated in the White Paper might reflect the desires of top management of the firms but they did not reflect the practices of the recruiters on campus. I saw enough evidence to believe that this concern was well founded at the beginning of the 1990s. But by 1995 the situation was different. A transformation took place in the first half of the 1990s. Not only did individual recruiters look for different attributes in candidates, but also firms focused their recruiting on colleges and universities that had programs focused on the attributes they desired. The major factor in this transformation was economic reality, not the AECC. But, I believe the Commission had some effect by stimulating the dialog on the attributes desired by the firms.

The Commission had a task force focused specifically on the early employment experiences of accounting graduates. The Statement prepared by this task force and issued by the Commission in 1993 was discussed in chapter 6. In effect, the Statement suggests addressing the gap between student expectations and actual job experiences by managing both the expectations and the experiences. My impression is that little progress has been made on the former, but the tight labor market in the last few years has forced some improvement in the deployment of recent graduates. Again, the economy rather than the Commission was probably the driving force, but the Commission discussions about this issue at least focused more attention on the problem and how to address it.

I believe a major factor in the Commission's success was the decision by the sponsoring firms to work through rather than around the academic establishment. They were willing to listen to accounting faculty and administrators as well as admonish them. I admit to having the biases of an academic, but I believe that colleges and universities understand the education production function better than do most practitioners. Because practitioners have been through the educational experience, some think they fully understand how educational institutions should function. The sponsoring firms generally resisted this temptation to specify how their desired knowledge, skills, and abilities should be developed. They did not develop a "model curriculum." In the White Paper, they provided only guidelines, such as the "textbook-based, rule-intensive, lecture/problem style should not survive," "new methods must be explored," "the curriculum should encourage the use of a team approach," and "an efficient curriculum requires attention to integration." The restructuring of programs and curricula was left to the Commission and ultimately to individual colleges and universities.

At the same time that the change activities were left primarily to the academy, the Commission provided an opportunity to look at accounting programs from a broader perspective. Academics are sometimes too involved to see the flaws in their educational processes. The academy is also relatively isolated from market forces. While market forces had caused changes in accounting practice, the academy had been able to ignore many of those forces, at least in the short run. The AECC was a mechanism to bring those market forces to the accounting academy. The sponsoring firms made it clear that the academy did not have a choice on whether to change, only on how to change.

Public Accounting Practitioners—Small and Mid-Sized Firms

While the large public accounting firms were instigators of change in accounting education, most small and mid-sized firms were not directly involved. The Commission had a representative from non-Big 8 firms, first Marvin Strait and then Jim Naus, and neither was reticent about expressing his views. But the variety of small and mid-sized firms made it impossible for a single voice to represent them. Thus, it was possible that the education advocated by the AECC was not appropriate for students wishing to enter many types of small and mid-sized CPA firms.

Critics of the approach to accounting education taken by the Bedford Committee, the White Paper, and the AECC were quick to point out that the day-to-day tasks of small accounting practitioners are quite different from those in large, international firms. From this they conclude that the education for small practitioners should also be different. The AECC disagreed. Although the Commission's reasoning on this was never made explicit, I believe the following is a reasonably close rendition.

Accounting practitioners need both education and training. Although the line between education and training is often blurry, the former focuses more on understanding and the latter on doing. Accounting programs at colleges and universities include both education and training. The training makes graduates valuable immediately on graduation, while education equips them to adapt their training to new situations, providing more value in the long run. The changes in accounting education in the 1990s are generally toward more education, with the necessary result being less training.

Education involves learning to think, communicate, and interact with others, and it also includes a conceptual understanding of the production and use of accounting information. Once learned, these capabilities last a lifetime. On the other hand, training involves learning and applying rules, regulations, techniques, and processes. These are valuable, but in an ever-changing world, they have a short half-life.

The major purpose of colleges and universities is education, not training. However, professional programs such as accounting must also include some training. Education without training does not prepare one for entry to the accounting profession. A brilliant physicist who can eloquently communicate the laws of physics cannot audit financial statements without training in accounting.

Likewise, training without education does not prepare one for a professional career. Although some accounting graduates may become accounting clerks because of their training, they are not the types of professionals that colleges and universities are supposed to produce. Only training that is paired with a good education, so that the training can be adapted as the professional environment changes, is useful to a true professional accountant.

The real issue in the current revolution in accounting education is the balance between education and training. The expansion in the field of accounting, in both scope and depth, and the accelerating pace of change in the profession have made education relatively more important than training. One reaction to this trade-off between education and training is to require more years of postsecondary education—five years instead of four. This can allow the education component to increase without a decrease in training. But the Commission elected to not enter the debate about length of accounting programs, but weighed in with a recommendation that a higher proportion of the time be devoted to education, whatever the length of the program.

To get back to the issue of the needs of small vs. large accounting firms, the question to ask is whether the required balance of education and training is different for small and large firms. Because of the variety of types of small accounting firms, it is hard to give a definitive answer. Firms that primarily compile and review financial statements for small companies, or those that primarily prepare tax returns, probably need entry-level accountants who have more training and less education. Those that provide a broad spectrum of consulting advice to a variety of clients probably require relatively more education.

Regardless of the type of accounting one practices, to be regarded as a professional implies an ability to continue to function in that capacity into the future, even as the economic landscape changes. Therefore, accounting graduates need at least a minimal amount of education (as opposed to training), and I believe the Commission would maintain that the minimum level is greater than that provided by many traditional accounting programs. Even graduates seeking positions in small firms will benefit from the additional education, even if it means less training.

With the overwhelming trend toward requiring five years of postsecondary education to sit for the CPA examination, the potential conflict between needs of large and small public accounting firms becomes less significant, at least for the present. In five years, there is probably enough time to add the needed education without decreasing the amount of training. Another trend that may decrease the difference between needs of large and small firms is the growing use of paraprofessionals. For positions that require primarily training, those for which environmental changes lead to retraining rather than adaptation, we will see more use of paraprofessionals. In this context, some graduates of accounting programs may become paraprofessionals rather than professionals, but university-level professional programs should not cater to such career goals.

In summary, the type of public accounting firm that graduates aspire to, large or small, should have only a small effect on the type of education provided to them. The exception would be states where four-year graduates can become CPAs; in those states the education required of a professional should probably dominate the undergraduate program. Thus, the Commission's recommendations would still apply.

Accounting Practitioners in Business, Industry, and Government

The AECC heard the views of business and industry from two Commission members, one each representing the Financial Executives Institute (first Steve Berlin and then Penny Flugger) and the Institute of Management Accountants (first John Chironna and then Stan Pylipow). There was no voice of government accountants on the Commission, although the Commission did have a session with Cornelius Tierney, National Director, Public Sector Practice, Ernst & Young, and Virginia Robinson, Executive Director, Joint Financial Management Program, on the need to include the topics of government accounting and auditing in the accounting curriculum. While the input from business, industry, and government was less than that from public accounting, the Commission was careful not to ignore their needs.

As described in chapter 1, one of the first actions of the Commission was to broadly define "accounting careers" and "accounting profession," including careers in public accounting, corporate accounting, and governmental and nonprofit accounting. In fact, the initial discussion of this issue came up in the early moments of the Commission's first meeting when Doyle Williams introduced its charge. The minutes of the meeting read as follows: "Members expressed concern that the commission might focus too much on education for public accounting and slight other accounting careers. The Commission decided to establish a task force to prepare a draft of the Commission's position on the breadth of accounting careers being considered." That task force prepared the Statement that very broadly defined accounting careers.

Despite efforts to incorporate all accounting careers, the Commission nevertheless was criticized for being too public-accounting oriented. Davis and Sherman (1994, 26) said that "the views of 'other stakeholders' have been discounted" by the AECC. Poe and Bushong (1991, 66) were more specific: "[Position Statement No. One] recognizes the broad diversity of knowledge within the profession but paradoxically calls for one curriculum to meet the needs of all areas." They go on to advocate specialized programs for various career objectives. Despite the fact that Position Statement No. One does not suggest any specific curriculum, Poe and Bushong (1991) are right that the Commission envisaged a common education for all accountants. According to the Commission, the skills, knowledge, and abilities in Position Statement No. One are necessary for whatever type of professional accounting career a person seeks. Specific career paths might warrant additional specialized education and training, but the Commission believed that the basic education upon which specializations are built is the same for all accounting careers.

The educational changes advocated by the AECC are consistent with many of the findings of studies dealing with the preparation of management accountants. For example, Novin et al. (1990, 213) reported: "A majority of the CMA respondents rated thinking, problem solving, and listening skills as extremely important. In addition, a majority felt that, if necessary, some study of accounting concepts and procedures should be sacrificed to provide for the development of these other skills." When asked what areas of accounting could be reduced, the conclusion was: "In general, while respondents approved of reducing the procedural aspect of some areas, they showed a greater reluctance to reduce the conceptual component of any of these categories" (Novin et al. 1990, 218).

A 1994 study sponsored by the Institute of Management Accountants and the Financial Executives Institute, *What Corporate America Wants in Entry-Level Accountants: Executive Summary* (Siegel and Sorensen 1994), adds further support to AECC initiatives. The report was released to great fanfare and misleading headlines (the press release was called "Colleges are not Adequately Preparing Accounting Graduates for first Jobs, Say Corporate Executives" [IMA 1994] and the *Wall Street Journal* headline read "College Courses on Accounting Get Poor Grade" [Berton 1994]), and it was used by some to chastise accounting education. Although the negative spin put on the results was not totally consistent with the data,[7] the report did highlight changes needed in the education of management accountants. Some of the failings of graduates cited (Siegel and Sorenson 1994, 4) were "lack of practical experience, little understanding of the 'big picture' or how the 'real world' works, and poor communication and social skills." Based on previous studies, the study took as given that "employers value a broad educational background and good social and communications skills." The directions of change advocated by the AECC were certainly consistent with the changes desired by corporate America.

The Institute of Management Accountants produced additional evidence consistent with AECC changes in a study of core competencies required for success in management accounting careers. The top ten competencies were (in order): work commitment, professional conduct, professional development, interpersonal skills, proactive skills, listening skills, team leadership and teamwork,

---

[7] The interpretations were also contrary to a more recent study by Accountemps (1998, 14) that showed that 88 percent of chief financial officers are either very satisfied or somewhat satisfied with the skill level of recent accounting and finance college graduates, compared to 12 percent who were either somewhat dissatisfied or very dissatisfied.

financial reporting, written communication skills, and strategic planning. Again, the competencies desired are consistent with those emphasized by the AECC.

In my view, most of the criticism of the AECC with relation to its effect on management accounting was misplaced. Management accountants, as well as public accountants, must shed the green-eye-shade, number-crunching image and focus on the interpretation of economic information and providing value-added services. The changes advocated by the Commission all move education in this direction.

The main failing of the Commission in this area may have been not stressing enough its opposition to the emphasis on rules, regulations, and standards in many traditional accounting programs. This emphasis gave accounting programs a financial-accounting orientation, even specifically a CPA-examination orientation, which did not meet the needs of business and industry. The Commission definitely weighed in against such an orientation, but it did not do much to promote its opposition as a benefit to students entering business or government. Further, the Commission's inability to gain much recognition of its activities among practicing accountants in business, industry, and government did not help. This may have been an impossible task because most such accountants are focused on serving their organization, not hiring new accountants. Nevertheless, the change process would have progressed better with more support from these sectors, and I believe that those who fully understood the goals of the Commission would have been enthusiastic supporters.

Business School and University Administrators

The Commission made extensive efforts to communicate with university and business school administrators, with only modest success. Several of the Commission's publications were sent to university administrators and business school deans in addition to accounting faculty and administrators. Support of top administrators was an important factor in the decisions to award grants to an institution. Although I know of no empirical evidence on the recognition of AECC activities by university administrators, my impression is that few university presidents and provosts would know of the Commission's work. I heard anecdotes of provosts or other top university officials forwarding AECC publications to the accounting chair apparently without reading them. Rather than the Commission enlisting top university officials to promote change in accounting, it was often incumbent on accounting faculty to sell change to their administrations.

Recognition among business school deans was greater, but I think most Commission members would agree that even here the AECC fell short of its goal. Several presentations were made to annual meetings of AACSB-The International Association for Management Education. These included hosting a breakfast session at the 1996 AACSB Annual Meeting to attract large numbers of deans. The vast majority of deans were familiar with the AECC, but the deans did not become great champions of AECC-supported changes. My impression was that the deans were not opposed to changes sought by the Commission, but their attention was mainly focused elsewhere.

It is unfortunate that more deans did not embrace AECC initiatives. All business school curricula, especially M.B.A. programs, were undergoing change at the same time as was accounting. Lessons learned from changes in accounting could be applied elsewhere. Especially useful were the monographs on intentional learning and assessment (Francis et al. 1995; Gainen and Locatelli 1995). Although these monographs tended to use accounting examples, they apply equally well to all areas of the business curriculum. Some colleges and universities used changes in accounting as leverage in generating changes across the entire business school curriculum and achieved great synergy by doing so.

Even if business school deans did not jump on the AECC bandwagon, they nevertheless provided an important mechanism for implementing parts of the AECC agenda—accreditation. At first the Commission regarded business and accounting accreditation as an impediment to change.

Traditional accreditation standards forced a cookie-cutter approach to business education. Accreditation standards represented one model of business education, and conformance with this model was necessary to join the "club" of accredited schools. But, by fortuitous timing, the AACSB was examining its accreditation standards at the time of formation of the AECC.

Accrediting Agencies

The forces that caused the formation of the AECC were affecting all of business education. The AACSB sponsored the Porter and McKibben (1988) study and, based on the results, it undertook a major revision of accreditation standards. The timing was perfect for AECC influence, and the Commission took full advantage of the opportunity.

By the late 1980s business accreditation had become a deterrent to innovation and change. An increasingly complex and diverse business world was being served by an academy that motivated conformity through accreditation standards. When the Porter and McKibben (1988) report made it clear that major changes were needed in business education, the AACSB found it necessary to revise accreditation standards to allow, and indeed encourage, change. A call for input to the revision process was presented at the AECC's first meeting, and a task force was immediately appointed to draft the Commission's position on accreditation.

The Commission's first discussion of accreditation contained a debate on whether separate accounting accreditation (in addition to business accreditation) was necessary. This discussion was reprised at the second, third, and fourth meetings of the Commission. At the third meeting, Rick Elam and Chuck Carpenter presented a list of pros and cons of accounting accreditation. Although some members continued to oppose accounting accreditation, the Commission formally voted at its fourth meeting to assume that there will be accounting accreditation and to use it as one tool for accomplishing its objectives. This is a good example of how the Commission carried forth a united front. The Commission's clout could have been used successfully to oppose and thereby possibly eliminate accounting accreditation, which was a goal of some Commission members. However, once the Commission made the decision to use accreditation rather than oppose it, all effort was put into making accreditation standards consistent with the AECC's objectives.

As the final stage of a long process, at its April 1991 meeting, the Commission voted to support the report of the AACSB Accreditation Task force that was being presented to the AACSB membership for approval. A formal resolution read as follows:

> The Accounting Education Change Commission expresses its deep appreciation to the AACSB Accreditation Project Task Force for: 1) Providing a timely opportunity for the Commission to respond to the work of the Accreditation Task Force: 2) Providing the opportunity for the Commission to engage in an active dialogue with representatives of the Accreditation Task Force; and 3) The Task Force's responsiveness to the recommendation of the Commission.

However, the path leading to this endorsement was not always smooth.

Although the Commission prepared and revised a letter of input to the AACSB Accreditation Task Force during its first three meetings, its view of accreditation really began to take shape during a discussion with Don Skadden during the meeting in February 1990. He presented the goals of the Task Force as: (1) to recognize the wide variety of business programs; (2) encourage improvement, innovation, and experimentation in programs; and (3) relate accreditation to an institution's goals. The Commission agreed with the goals. However, differences of opinion arose when discussing how to achieve these goals.

A major area of disagreement was the Task Force's suggestion that colleges and universities be accredited in one of four categories: (1) Teaching, (2) Graduate Teaching, (3) Graduate Research, and (4) Research. The AACSB Task Force placed no hierarchical relation on these categories, but Commission members seemed convinced that the perception would be that a research accreditation is the "best" accreditation to have, while a teaching accreditation is the lowest. Such a system would motivate a shift of resources from teaching to research in order to "progress" up the hierarchy. The interchange with Skadden was spirited and very useful. At the end, the Commission was resolutely opposed to the four-way categorization. Instead, it suggested that each institution should be judged against its own goals and objectives.

Although opposition to categorization of accreditation was the most passionate point made by the Commission, other suggestions included:

- The need to use longitudinal measures to show continuous improvement;
- The need to review accreditation on a more timely basis, possibly every three years;
- Opposition to accreditation of Ph.D. programs.

After further discussion with Don Skadden in June 1990, it was clear that the Commission and the AACSB Task Force were moving closer to a common view. However, the prospect of accreditation categories had not yet been exorcised, so the Commission prepared another Statement for the Task Force.

By January 1991, the AACSB Task Force had issued another draft that addressed many of the Commission's concerns. The Commission chose to comment on only two additional issues. First was Ph.D. program accreditation. It was clear that its recommendation to exempt Ph.D. programs from accreditation would not be accepted. But two requirements for Ph.D. programs present in an earlier draft had been dropped, and the AECC wanted to see them reinserted. The first called for a breath-of-knowledge requirement and the second for instruction in teaching and curriculum development. In relation to the second requirement, an AECC survey revealed that only 17 of 56 Ph.D. programs offered a course in how to teach, and only 10 of them were required. The Commission wanted an incentive for universities to provide instruction in teaching and course and curriculum development as a routine part of doctoral programs.

The other issue was the first course in accounting. The proposed standards exempted introductory accounting from the standards for academically qualified faculty. This course is very important, and the Commission felt that it was important to motivate the use of qualified faculty in it. The final standards accommodated both of these recommendations, albeit it in different words than those suggested by the Commission.

In summary, revision of the AACSB accreditation standards was well under way before the AECC was formed. Nevertheless, the Commission's positions on several accreditation issues led to additional revisions in the proposed standards. Whether any of these revisions would have been made in the absence of the Commission's input is impossible to determine. However, I think it is safe to say that the final standards were significantly different than they would have been if the Commission had not had an influence. (For more information on how the new accreditation standards affect accounting programs see Bailey [1994].)

Chapter 8
MEASURING AND ASSESSING CHANGE

From its first meeting, the AECC was concerned with measuring the impacts of educational changes. In fact, two task forces addressed measurement. One task force focused on how to measure the impact of program changes on the skills and capabilities of students, and the other focused on measuring the role of the Commission itself in bringing about changes in accounting programs.

Measuring Changes in Student Capabilities

Changes in educational processes are often accepted simply on the basis of logic and *ex ante* reasoning. The Commission wanted more evidence that changes being undertaken in accounting programs truly generated increased capabilities in students. This concern was evident in many of the Commission's activities. Grant proposals were required to specify plans for measuring the impacts of program revisions. Such assessment plans were thoroughly discussed in evaluating proposals. Several meetings were held so that representatives of the grant schools could compare notes on their assessment plans and activities. For one of these meetings, all grant recipients were asked to write a two-page document on the methods used (or proposed) to measure outcomes. Site visits by the AECC liaisons included discussions of the measurement of outcomes. Nevertheless, outcome assessment remained an elusive topic.

The need for assessment was not unique to accounting programs. Educational institutions had focused for years on measuring inputs; measuring outputs, and especially outcomes, did not come easily. Accountability and related assessment was a rallying cry in all of education, from kindergarten to graduate programs. Whether imposed by government agencies or initiated internally, nearly all educational institutions were undertaking some kind of assessment. The Commission believed that accountants, with their expertise in measurement, could lead the way in educational assessment. Therefore, the AECC undertook its own project in assessment.

A well-received monograph was the result: *Assessment for the New Curriculum: A Guide for Professional Accounting Programs,* by Joanne Gainen and Paul Locatelli. Published in 1995, this monograph provides background on the assessment movement in the United States. It outlines a model for developing an assessment program and provides guidance for faculty to assess not only the traditional learning outcomes, but also the expanded learning outcomes advocated by the AECC and others. It also illustrates the use of assessment as a tool for continuous improvement of learning outcomes and client satisfaction.

The Process of Change

The process of change is seldom smooth. The accounting education changes in the 1990s were no exception. The process of change undertaken by the Commission had three main phases: (1) create acceptance of the need for change, (2) develop the direction of change and the means of achieving it, and (3) implement the changes throughout accounting programs in the United States. I don't think this three-pronged approach was ever explicit in the strategy of the Commission, but it is a logical way to summarize the process. All three phases began in the early stages of the Commission's life, and they were accomplished nearly sequentially.

The Commission did not have to convince faculty of the need for change as much as to emphasize its urgency. As mentioned earlier, changes in accounting programs had been discussed for years. In the 1980s it became clear that something needed to be done. The Commission focused on coalescing opinions on what changes to make and the necessity to make them sooner rather than later.

A factor that made change especially difficult was the magnitude of the required change. Accounting education flourished in the 1970s and early 1980s. Accounting programs kept attracting more and better students. The marketplace seemed to have an insatiable demand for accounting graduates. Some years were better than others were, but the over-all trend was always positive. Programs were growing and external funding was steadily increasing. Accounting programs seemed isolated from the profession's rocky roads of litigation and increasing competition. The prevailing view in accounting academe, though seldom explicitly articulated, seemed to be "don't rock the boat."

Accounting faculty were not blind to the need to continually evolve their programs. In fact the 1970s and 1980s were times of great change in the accounting research programs in most schools. A growing number of colleges and universities instituted research and publication requirements for their faculty, and these requirements seemed to be continually increasing. Unfortunately, much of the research program changes did not affect the teaching programs. Contrary to the synergy between teaching and research that drove the development of the research universities after World War II, the growth of research in accounting seemed to be parallel to, not integrated with, teaching. Nevertheless, accounting departments were quite different in 1990 from what they were in 1970.

At the same time, certain segments of the accounting curriculum also underwent major changes. The teaching of auditing is a major example, moving in most universities from a focus on how to do an audit to an understanding of the audit process. A similar move to a more conceptual orientation took place in many tax courses. However, the core of the accounting curriculum— financial and management accounting—experienced little change.

The Commission interpreted the slow pace of change in accounting curricula as a sign of complacency in the accounting academy. A majority of the Commission felt that a bold step was necessary to break through this complacency. This led to the most controversial action taken by the Commission, the issuance of Issues Statement No. 1, *AECC Urges Priority for Teaching in Higher Education*. The Statement upset some members of the accounting academic community—an outcome that was both good and bad. A wake-up call was needed, and the Statement grabbed the attention of most faculty. However, by antagonizing a segment of the accounting academic community that could have been leaders in developing the needed changes, it also hindered the process of change.

While Issues Statement No. 1 was an attention-grabber, a more grass-roots effort, which involved speaking at a large number of conferences and universities and publishing various articles, was also an important part of selling the need for change. A combination of Commission efforts and market forces led to widespread acceptance of the need to change by the early 1990s.

The direction of change was set primarily by the Commission's Position Statement No. One, *Objectives of Education for Accountants*. Methods of change were developed primarily by the grant schools. Yet, it is clear that the Commission did not have a monopoly on ideas for and models of change. Many colleges and universities proceeded with change activities independent of AECC support. Some received support elsewhere. For example, Coopers & Lybrand supported changes at the University of Southern California, and California State University, Chico received government funding from FIPSE (Fund for the Improvement of Postsecondary Education). But the majority tackled change activities with no outside funding. Some of these efforts were described in the special AECC issues of *Accounting Education News*, but the majority were simply program improvements that did not receive notice outside the college or university implementing them.

Would models of change have arisen without the AECC? Probably many of them would have. But the Commission created projects that had an explicit obligation to widely share their change experiences with others. In addition, the Commission helped create an atmosphere where curriculum change and experimentation were viewed more positively than previously. Finally, the Commission provided forums for sharing experiences, speeding the process of learning what might work and what might not work.

The final phase, widespread implementation of changes, is an ongoing process. Few colleges and universities have not made some changes in their curricula. But so far, the widespread changes have been primarily those that were easy to accomplish rather than those with the greatest long-term benefit. Pedagogy has changed more than content. I believe that the success of the AAA's faculty and program development activities will play a major role in the successful implementation of the more fundamental changes needed. Changing faculty capabilities and their comfort with new approaches to the teaching of accounting is essential to implementing the changes. While the AECC set the stage for this phase, its accomplishment is beyond the Commission's purview.

One benchmark for judging the widespread implementation of AECC-supported changes is changes in textbooks. On the surface, the Commission has had a noticeable affect on accounting textbooks. Almost every introductory accounting text has a section in the preface telling how it meets AECC suggestions. End-of-chapter materials invariably include problems, exercises, and cases designed to foster problem-solving, communication, and team-building skills. But, like most accounting programs, most textbooks have addressed the easy changes and have ignored the more fundamental ones. Some texts with significantly different approaches—most consistent with AECC objectives—have been published, but they generally have not made major inroads in the marketplace.

One positive factor from the textbook market is revealed in Sullivan and Benke (1997). They categorized introductory financial accounting textbooks from traditional to revolutionary (where revolutionary books are generally more consistent with AECC objectives), and then asked authors to comment on the categorization. Most authors did not agree with their categorization, and all but one author thought his or her book should be ranked further toward the revolutionary end of the scale. From this, Sullivan and Benke (1997, 199) concluded, "authors are trying to move toward the Revolutionary category." If this attitude carries over into their next revisions, textbooks will gradually incorporate more of the Commission's suggestions, and the entire accounting textbook market will move in that direction. On the other hand, if authors already believe that their text is more revolutionary than it is, maybe they will not see the need to move further in that direction.

Resistance to Change

The process of change is not easy. Often those with the most at stake are the most resistant to changes. This was the case with accounting education changes. Faculty, students, and parents all had reasons for opposing change. Change agents need to anticipate this opposition and develop strategies to deal with it. Lessons on resistance to change learned primarily from the experience of the grant schools were presented to the Commission by a committee of the Federation of Schools of Accountancy in August 1993. A related paper (Pincus et al. 1993) reported the results. I will summarize only the main points in this section.

Faculty were the most threatened by the changes. Among the reasons for their resistance are:

- They do not agree with the reasons for change.
  - Reluctance to change programs that have worked well in the past.
  - Mixed signals from practice on what is desired.
  - Changes will leave students less well prepared for CPA examination.

- They fear an inability to succeed in a changed environment.
  - ° Loss of "ownership" of classes.
  - ° Skills, such as dynamic lecturing, may not be rewarded in the future.
  - ° Feel incompetent to teach broader skills.[8]
- They resist the great effort required to change.
  - ° Familiar textbooks will be replaced with new ones.
  - ° Curricular reform takes much effort and offers little reward.
  - ° University approval processes are long and time-consuming.
  - ° Lack of administrative and resource support for changes.
- They wish to avoid conflict with faculty with opposing views.
  - ° Integrated curriculum requires agreement across faculty.
  - ° Lack of cooperation of faculty outside of accounting.

Student concerns centered on how the changes would affect their chances of success in accounting courses and in an accounting career:

- Change brings uncertainty in expectations.
  - ° Unknown level of difficulty in the new curriculum.
  - ° New program differs greatly from expectations developed in high school accounting classes and from previous accounting students.
  - ° Learning in teams conflicts with the methods learned to compete against each other.
  - ° Rumors bring fear of the unknown, especially if some faculty express reservations about the changes.
  - ° Materials are more varied and are not always available in standard (textbook) format.
- The fear of uncertainty is especially great in grading.
  - ° Grading on communications and team exercises adds subjectivity.
  - ° Loss of control over grades as expectations change.
  - ° Textbooks do not provide a boundary around what is expected to be learned.
- The fear that they will be less prepared to succeed in the accounting profession.
  - ° Not be technically competent to pass the CPA (or CMA or CIA) examination.
  - ° Mixed signals from recruiters about the new curriculum.

Student resistance to change was especially strong when a pilot program was tested. The students in the pilot program were often concerned that they were not learning the traditional materials that their peers in the regular curriculum learned. Those in the traditional curriculum felt they were not getting as much attention as were those in the pilot program. This resulted in unhappy students in both groups.

The good thing about student resistance is that it generally disappears after about three years of experience with the revised curriculum. Students turn over every year, so in a short period of time the collective student body has no knowledge about how the program used to be. The "new" curriculum is no longer new to them—it is just what is expected.

In some programs, resistance to change came from an unexpected source—parents of students. Two factors seemed to bring this out: (1) parents whose children did not do well in the new curriculum, and (2) parents who studied accounting themselves and were concerned that their children were not learning the technical detail that they did as students.

---

[8] This fear was articulated by Richards (1992, 15): "Certainly accounting educators can teach the base level of skills, but can we teach the second-level skills? It is difficult to see how we can, either now or ever....We do not have the education in these areas, and it is not likely that we ever will. If skills beyond the base level are to be taught, they should not, indeed cannot, be taught by the accounting faculty....Accounting educators are teachers of accounting and nothing more." This is a very pessimistic view of the capabilities of accounting faculty.

Overcoming Resistance to Change

There are many things that can be done to overcome resistance to change, if change is correctly anticipated. Most important is to make sure that everyone has full information. Many schools have found it worthwhile to bring in outside experts, recruiters, employers, and alumni to address both faculty and students on the need for change and how the changes are likely to improve the program. Both written and oral communication to students is an obvious step, but communication with faculty, including those outside accounting is often overlooked. Sometimes such communication comes only after resistance is encountered, which often is too late.

Communication with students, their parents, high school and two-year-college counselors, employers, and others affected by the changes should take the form of a marketing campaign. Not only will this reduce misinformation, it will focus on the strengths and benefits of the revised program to students entering the business world. Especially important is bringing employers and alumni to the classroom and other student events to address how the changes will affect students after they graduate and enter the job market.

In addition to mere communication, participation in the change process is important. For faculty this is probably obvious. If faculty are to change how they teach, they need to be involved in determining how such changes will be decided and implemented. But other stakeholder involvement can also help the change process. Advisory boards are especially valuable because they bring the perspective of the marketplace to the deliberations. Students might be represented on planning committees, but more important is the use of student focus groups to react to planned changes. Not only will this provide insights into where student resistance may be encountered and how the program might be designed to minimize such resistance, it will often yield a set of informed students who can sell the concept of change to the other students.

Providing support to both faculty and students is also important, and it can be one of the most expensive parts of the change process. Faculty support comes mainly during the planning phases. Retreats, training sessions, and sending faculty to programs that will enhance their skills are ways of providing support. At some point, the hiring of an independent mediator may be helpful. Incentive schemes that reward faculty for devoting the time and effort needed to participate in the change process are powerful but possibly expensive methods of support. Some schools find that providing release time from other obligations, bonuses, or summer support for curriculum development is sufficient reward; others add a curriculum development component to faculty performance evaluation systems. Protection from low student evaluations when experimenting with curricular change is also helpful.

Student support includes a good orientation program, an open-door policy for counseling and guidance, open discussion sessions where students can voice their concerns and suggest improvements, and extra help in areas not traditionally considered part of the accounting curriculum. For the latter, writing centers are a very common support facility provided.

Sometimes gaining acceptance of changes requires negotiated compromises. Reduced class size might be the cost of getting a changed curriculum. Keeping some traditional materials may be necessary to introduce some new materials. Nontenured faculty might be protected from the efforts of curriculum revision so that they can devote their effort to the research necessary for promotion. In some cases, a small number of faculty may be exempted from the change activities and allowed to teach some courses using traditional methods so that they do not undercut the entire change process. All of these may reduce the complete commitment to change, but they may be necessary to accomplish any change at all.

Compromises on the student side usually involve allowing choices between old and new courses during a transition period. Students who choose to participate in a new curriculum have already made a step toward accepting change.

Resistance is a natural part of the change process, and it can be healthy as well as an obstacle. By anticipating and dealing with resistance, programs can alter plans to accommodate legitimate concerns and overcome some of the obstacles that are potential threats to change.

AECC in the Literature—Publications

One measure of the impact of the AECC is the degree to which articles by or about the Commission appear in the accounting literature and the number of times AECC publications are cited. By these measures, it is clear that the Commission has at least been noticed by authors and readers of the literature.

One way the AECC tried to reach a variety of audiences was through publications. Both of the Position Statements and the first four Issues Statements were published in *Issues in Accounting Education* before being collected in a special volume published by the AAA (AECC 1996). In addition, the Commission published three articles describing the grant proposals that were accepted for publication (Williams and Sundem 1990, 1991; Williams 1992c).

Listing all publications by all Commission members that made reference to the Commission would be a waste of space. However, some examples should suffice. The Chairman and Executive Director wrote many short pieces for a variety of newsletters (e.g. Williams 1992a, 1992b; Sundem 1991b, 1991c, 1991d). They also addressed practitioner and student audiences (e.g., Chironna et al. 1990; Sundem 1991a; Williams 1993). Many other Commission members also carried forth the message in print (e.g., Elliott 1992; Elliott and Jacobson 1992; Kieso 1992a, 1992b; Strait 1992).

In the later years of the Commission, the grant schools carried much of the publication burden. Some of the grant school publications are listed in exhibit 8-1. These publications are in addition to the descriptions published by the AECC (Williams and Sundem 1990, 1991; Williams 1992c; Flaherty 1998). Although not officially "published," the average grant school also provided written information about its project to more than 70 parties that requested such information. In addition, several put information on their web sites.

AECC in the Literature—Citations

Citations to the AECC in the accounting education literature have been extensive.[9] Citations began appearing in about 1992, and they have been relatively constant through mid-1998. To assess the extent of these citations, I examined the two largest accounting education journals, *Issues in Accounting Education* and *Journal of Accounting Education*. From 1992 through mid-1998, 47 percent of the main articles (107 out of 229 articles) referred to one or more AECC publications. (In the tally, I omitted cases and other special sections that had few, if any, citations to the literature.) There is little difference between the two journals, with 46 percent of the articles in *Issues in Accounting Education* citing the Commission and 48 percent of those in *Journal of Accounting Education*.

The number of citations has stayed relatively constant across time. From 1996 to mid-1998, 51 percent of the articles cited the Commission, compared with 43 percent from 1992 through 1995. Annual citation percentages are:

1992	1993	1994	1995	1996	1997	1998
38%	55%	32%	46%	53%	45%	56%

For the Commission to be cited in nearly 50 percent of the articles over a period of seven years is a clear indication that authors of the articles were paying attention to the Commission. And there is no indication that references to the Commission are declining—if anything they have increased slightly in later years. Thus, one would expect such citations to continue.

---

[9]   As expected, there are few citations of the AECC in the accounting *research* literature.

EXHIBIT 8-1
Publications by the AECC Grant Schools

Ainsworth, P. 1992. *Flint Hills Salon: A Case Analysis*. John Wiley & Sons.
———, and D. Plumlee. 1993. Restructuring the accounting curriculum content sequence: The KSU experience. *Issues in Accounting Education* (Spring): 112–127.
———. 1994. Restructuring the introductory accounting courses: The Kansas State University experience. *Journal of Accounting Education* (Fall): 305–323.
———, D. Deines, D. Plumlee, and C. Larson. 1997. *Introduction to Accounting: An Integrated Approach*. Richard D. Irwin.
Albrecht, S. 1991. Implementing a new curriculum: The BYU experience. *FSA Proceedings, 1991 Annual Meeting* (December): 95–102.
———. 1992. Education update on BYU's new curriculum. *Education Update* (Spring).
———, and J. Smith. 1993. Integrating auditing across the undergraduate curriculum. *Proceedings of Auditing Education Conference*, Lehigh University, May 20–21.
———, and ———. 1994. Integrating auditing across the curriculum. *Proceedings of Auditing Education Conference*, SUNY at Binghamton.
———, C. Clark, J. Smith, K. Stocks, and L. Woodfield. 1994. An accounting curriculum for the next century. *Issues in Accounting Education* (Fall): 401–425.
———. 1997. U.S. educators look to the big picture. *Australian Accountant* (May): 52–54.
Chronicle of Higher Education. 1997. The new accounting. (January 31): A10.
Cooper, W., G. Faucette, and C. Malone. 1995. Introducing practical experience into accounting education. *Accounting Forum* (March): 69–78.
———, L. Griffin, and C. Malone. 1996. Advisory Services Ltd.: An interdisciplinary project involving accounting and technology students. *Mid-American Journal of Business* (Fall): 48–58.
DeMong, R., J. Lindgren, and S. Perry. 1994. Designing an assessment program for accounting. *Issues in Accounting Education* (Spring): 11–27.
Deppe, L., E. Sonderegger, J. Stice, D. Clark, and F. Streuling. 1991. Emerging competencies for the practice of accountancy. *Journal of Accounting Education* (Fall): 257–290.
Hill, N., S. Perry, and D. Stein. 1998. Using accounting student surveys in an outcomes assessment program. *Issues in Accounting Education* (February): 65–78.
Insight. 1995–1996. Educators stop spoon feeding students. (December –January): 20–24.
Jones, K., J. Price, M. Werner, and M. Doran. 1996. *Introduction to Financial Accounting: A User Perspective*. Prentice-Hall.
Lewis, C. 1995. Critical thinking and the introductory accounting curriculum. *American Accounting Association Communicator* (February): 17–18.
Pattison, D., P. McKenzie, and R. Birney. 1995. *Interactive Managerial Accounting Lab*. McGraw Hill.
Romney, M., J. O. Cherrington, and E. L. Denna. 1996. Using information systems as a basis for teaching accounting. *Journal of Accounting Education* (Spring): 57–68.
Smith, R., and R. Birney. 1995. *Interactive Financial Accounting Lab*. McGraw Hill.
Stone, D., and J. Shelley. 1997. Educating for accounting expertise: A field study. *Journal of Accounting Research* (Supplement): 35–61.

By far the most-often cited publication is Position Statement No. One, *Objectives of Education for Accountants*. Of the 107 articles citing the Commission, 82 percent cite the *Objectives* Statement. Next most often cited is Position Statement No. Two, *The First Course in Accounting*, cited by 17 percent of the 107 articles. The only other AECC publications with more than five citations are Issues Statement No. 1, *AECC Urges Priority for Teaching in Higher Education*, and Issues Statement No. 5, *Evaluating and Rewarding Effective Teaching*.

Beyond the U. S. Accounting Literature

Although the Commission's main goal was to affect accounting education, its activities reached beyond the borders of accounting. For example, Jean Wyer's article in *Change* magazine (Wyer 1993) introduced the Commission and its activities to a broad, interdisciplinary audience. The Commission has also been referenced in academic business journals outside accounting such as *Journal of Applied Business Research* and *Business Communications Quarterly.*

International journals have also shown interest in articles on the AECC. The British journal *Accounting Education* includes many references to the AECC, including two full articles. Sundem and Williams (1992) described the basis for the changes advocated by the Commission. Later, Mathews (1994) described the activities of the Commission, criticisms of its activities, and implications for other countries. He concluded that "there is a very high level of support for the work of the AECC" and that the grant program "as a whole appears to be working although it will take several more years to establish whether the entire scheme has been a success" (Mathews 1994, 200, 202). Journals in several other countries, including Canada, Ireland, Germany, Japan and New Zealand, have also had articles on the Commission.

Awards to AECC Grant Projects

One measure of the quality of the AECC grant projects is the awards they have received. Three of the projects have won the AAA Innovation in Accounting Education Award: 1993—Brigham Young University School of Accountancy & Information Systems; 1995—School of Accountancy, Arizona State University; and 1997—David Croll and Anthony Catanach, Jr. The first two are self-explanatory, but the third needs a bit of elaboration.

David Croll and Anthony Catanach, Jr. are on the faculty of the McIntire School at the University of Virginia. They developed a new approach to the intermediate accounting course as part of Virginia's AECC grant project. Their "Business Activity Model" (BAM) replaced the traditional lectures and textbook assignments of intermediate accounting with a two-semester focus on accounting for a business from its inception through seven years of operation. Jensen (1998) calls their approach "revolutionary," and indicates that "the BAM approach makes students search for answers on their own or in teams....The main innovation of the BAM pedagogy is that students teach themselves in a discovery learning pedagogy."

Chapter 9
CONCLUSION

The Accounting Education Change Commission began its seven-year life in 1989. By the time it handed off its activities to the American Accounting Association in 1996, it had made its mark on accounting education. The role of the Commission was to be a catalyst for change, and it accomplished that goal admirably. *Webster's* defines a catalyst as "an agent that provokes or speeds significant change or action." The AECC both provoked and speeded change in accounting education. It did not cause that change—the environment was ripe for change when the AECC was appointed. But without the prodding and leadership of the Commission, change would have been slower and possibly quite different.

Despite the efforts and successes of the AECC, however, the change process in accounting education was not finished in 1996, and it continues today. The ultimate success of the Commission will not be measured by the activities it undertook, but by the nature of the accounting education programs in colleges and universities in the year 2000 and beyond.

The AECC used two approaches to encourage improvements in accounting education: (1) the power of persuasion, and (2) the power of the pocketbook. Neither approach alone could have achieved the Commission's objectives.

Persuasion had two distinct phases. In the early years of the Commission, it focused on convincing the academy (and, to some extent, practitioners) of the *need* for change. In the later years, attention shifted to conveying information about *how to improve* accounting programs. Extensive publishing and public speaking programs were combined with official pronouncements on issues deemed to be important to the change process. In addition, targeted workshops made details available to interested parties.

Several factors were responsible for the widespread impact of the Commission's persuasive efforts. First, the AECC had the resources and organizational structure to prepare and deliver a consistent and compelling message. Second, AECC members were respected representatives of the accounting academy and accounting practice and were generous in their time and efforts on behalf of the Commission's agenda. Third, the American Accounting Association, its Sections and Regions, and other organizations provided platforms, both written and oral, for the Commission's message. Finally, accounting faculty and administrators recognized both the threats and opportunities in a fast-changing environment and were receptive to exploring new educational approaches.

However, persuasion could go only so far. Committing financial resources to the change process was necessary, both (1) to gain the attention of those who would lead the change process and (2) to provide prototypes of change for those following. The grant program proved to be a good vehicle to accomplish both objectives. The AECC made 11 grants to 12 schools. As in most research and development investments, some were more successful than were others. But, in total, there were more successes than failures, and lessons were learned even from the less-successful projects.

The AECC was most successful in creating changes in accounting pedagogy, especially in promoting the development of communication and interpersonal skills in accounting curricula.

Significant progress was made in changing the content of accounting courses to be more consistent with the recommendations of the Bedford Committee report, but much remains to be done. Limited success was achieved in developing measures for assessment of accounting programs, despite much effort by the Commission and several grant schools. The lack of success in developing assessment measures leads to concerns about whether accounting programs have moved to an environment of continuous improvement. The Commission did not seek a single, one-time change in accounting education, but a change in process that would lead to constantly monitoring and adapting programs to meet changes in the professional and practicing environments. The AECC certainly helped break the inertia that impeded changes in accounting education in the last few decades, but it remains to be seen whether a new inertia is about to settle in.

The 1990s have been an unsettling but exciting time for accounting education. The Accounting Education Change Commission played a major role in defining and carrying out the agenda for change in accounting education that has been a hallmark of this decade. There may be disagreement about the extent of the AECC's role, or about the desirability of the changes promoted by the Commission, but it is hard to argue that accounting education was unaffected by the Commission.

As I mentioned early in this monograph, I am by no means an unbiased observer of the Commission and its impact. Nevertheless, I will venture a bottom-line assessment: The AECC, while not perfect, had a positive impact on accounting education that will be felt for years to come. I am proud to have played a part in it.

Appendix A
COMMISSION MEMBERS

Steven R. Berlin, 1989–1992.

Steve Berlin was nominated for the AECC by the Financial Executive Institute. He was on the Leadership Support, Student Recruiting, and Change Commission Progress Task Forces.

Mr. Berlin was Senior Vice President and Chief Financial Officer of CITGO Petroleum Corporation, a multibillion-dollar petroleum, refining, and marketing company based in Tulsa, Oklahoma. He held a variety of operational, administrative and financial positions during his years with CITGO. He has since retired and is on the faculty at the University of Tulsa.

Mr. Berlin has held several leadership positions with the American Institute of Certified Public Accountants and the Financial Executives Institute, including FEI's Committee on Education (which he currently chairs) and the Council of the AICPA. He has also served on and as Treasurer of the Accounting Accreditation Committee of the American Assembly of Collegiate Schools of Business.

Mr. Berlin is a graduate of Duquesne University and holds an M.B.A. from the University of Wisconsin–Madison. He has taught in the accounting departments at several universities during his career, including the University of Houston, Tulsa University, and the University of Wisconsin–Madison.

Mr. Berlin is active in numerous civic, business and professional organizations and speaks on the need for educational reforms around the country.

Sarah G. Blake, 1991–1996.

Sarah Blake was nominated for the AECC by the National Association of State Boards of Accountancy. She was the AECC liaison to the Mesa Community College grant project, chair of the Professional Examinations Task Force, a member of the Curriculum Dissemination Task Force, and a member of the Dissemination Conferences and Learning to Learn project teams.

Mrs. Blake is the President and Chief Executive Officer of the Technology Development and Management Co. Prior to her current position, Mrs. Blake served as the President and Chief Executive Officer of the Arizona Technology Development Corporation.

Mrs. Blake, a certified public accountant, has served the University of Arizona as Vice President for Planning and Budgeting, Associate Vice President for Finance, Assistant Vice President for Planning and Budgeting, and Director for Institutional Finance.

Mrs. Blake holds a B.S. (Accounting) from the University of Arizona. She has been President of the Arizona State Board of Accountancy and is immediate Past Chairman of the National Association of State Boards of Accountancy. She also has served NASBA as a regional director and as a member of the International Reciprocity and Quality Review Committees. She has also served on the National Advisory Council for Beta Alpha Psi. She has served on numerous AICPA and Arizona Society of CPA Committees, and is currently a member of the AICPA Board of Examiners.

Mrs. Blake has published numerous articles in national journals on the issues of high technology planning and valuation. She is on the Board of Directors of several profit technology businesses, as well as non-profit associations interested in high technology management issues.

John F. Chironna, 1989–1993.

John Chironna was nominated for the AECC by the Institute of Management Accountants. He was a member of the Leadership Support and Early Employment Experience Task Forces.

Mr. Chironna was President and Chief Executive officer of BroadCom, Inc. during his tenure on the Commission. Previously, he was employed by IBM for 28 years in several executive positions, including Corporate Director of Accounting Operations with worldwide responsibility. While at IBM, Mr. Chironna served on the Advisory Councils for both Rutgers University's School of Business and the University of Georgia's School of Accounting. Later he became one of the original members of the Emerging Issues Task Force of the FASB.

After retiring from IBM he served as Interim Executive Director of the Institute of Management Accountants (then called the National Association of Accountants). Mr. Chironna also served on the Advisory Council to the Financial Accounting Standards Board and was one of the two U.S. representatives to the International Accounting Standards Committee. In addition, he was a member of the Executive Committee and Board of Directors of the National Association of Accountants for eight years and member of the Board of Directors of the Federation of Schools of Accountancy for two years. Mr. Chironna's volunteer service at the IMA includes four years on the Management Accounting Practices Committee, three of those years as Chairman. While serving as Chairman he created the Promulgation Subcommittee, which issued the Definition and Objectives of Management Accounting and the Code of Ethics for Management Accountants. He also served on the editorial board of *New Accountant* magazine.

Mr. Chironna received his B.A.A. in Accounting from St. John's University and his M.B.A. in Accounting and Taxes from New York University.

Robert K. Elliott, 1989–1994.

Bob Elliott was a member of the Early Employment Experience, Instructional Materials, Accreditation, CPA Examination, and Measurement of Educational Change (later Assessment) Task Forces and the Screening Committee for grants. He was also the AECC liaison for the Rutgers University grant project and a member of the Learning to Learn project team and the Sponsors' Task Force. He had a leading role in the conception, formation, and funding of the Commission and his vision for accounting education and communication skills are evident in the Commission's pronouncements.

Mr. Elliott, a certified public accountant, is a partner in the National Office of KPMG Peat Marwick LLP in New York and is currently Assistant to the Chairman.

Mr. Elliott chaired the AICPA's Special Committee on Assurance Services and served as a member of the AICPA's Special Committee on Financial Reporting. He is a member of the AICPA Board of Directors and Governing Council and chairs the AICPA's Strategic Planning Committee. He is a past member of the AICPA Future Issues Committee and Auditing Standards Board. He is also a past Vice President of the American Accounting Association and a past member of its Executive Committee and Council. He is a recipient of the AICPA's Gold Medal Award for Distinguished Service and the American Accounting Association's Notable Contributions to the Accounting Literature, Wildman Medal Award, and Distinguished Service in Auditing Awards. Mr. Elliott has been a member of the editorial boards of *The Accounting Review*, *Auditing: A Journal of Practice & Theory*, *Accounting Horizons*, *The Harvard Business School Series in Accounting and Control*, and *The Journal of Accountancy*.

Mr. Elliott has an A.B. from Harvard College and an M.B.A. from Rutgers. His publications, as author or co-author, include five books and more than 70 articles.

Richard E. Flaherty, 1993–1996.

Rich Flaherty was Executive Director of the AECC, 1993–1996. He was the AECC liaison for the University of North Texas grant project and was a member of the Curriculum Dissemination Task Force.

Dr. Flaherty is Professor of Accounting and former Director of the School of Accountancy at Arizona State University. He received his B.S., M.S., and Ph.D. degrees from the University of Kansas. Dr. Flaherty previously served on the faculties of Oklahoma State University and the University of Illinois. He also served as a research associate at the Financial Accounting Standards Board, as a consultant on financial reporting issues to a number of businesses, and has taught in many professional development programs. He has published numerous articles on financial accounting theory and practice. In addition, he is the author of a textbook and Accounting Education Research Monograph No. 3, *The Core of the Curriculum for Accounting Majors*, published by the American Accounting Association.

Dr. Flaherty is a member of the American Accounting Association, American Institute of Certified Public Accountants, Financial Executives Institute, and the Arizona Society of Certified Public Accountants. He has served on the Board of Examiners of the AICPA and on numerous committees and task forces of the Board. He has also served on the Board of the AAA's Administrators of Accounting (now the Accounting Programs Leadership Group). He has chaired the Accounting Accreditation Committee and served as a member of the Candidacy Committee and the Peer Review Improvement Task Force of the American Assembly of Collegiate Schools of Business. He also chaired the AACSB's Peer Review Improvement Task Force and was a member of the Strategic Planning Oversight Committee. He has also been a member of the governing board of both the Administrators of Accounting Programs Group (now the Accounting Programs Leadership Group) and the Federation of Schools of Accountancy.

Penelope A. Flugger, 1992–1996.

Penny Flugger was nominated for the AECC by the Financial Executives Institute. She was the AECC liaison to the University of Virginia grant project and was a member of the Assessment Task Force and the VIP Contacts Project Team.

Ms. Flugger is a Managing Director of J. P. Morgan & Co. Incorporated. Ms. Flugger joined Morgan in 1975 as an Assistant Comptroller. She was assigned to Audit in 1981. In 1994 she assumed responsibility for control and quality initiatives in Morgan's technology and operations group. Before joining Morgan, Ms. Flugger was with Price Waterhouse, where she served as an audit manager.

Ms. Flugger received a B.S. degree from the University of Illinois in 1964 and, in the same year, became a Certified Public Accountant. She received an M.B.A. from Baruch College–City University of New York in 1971.

Ms. Flugger is a member of the Financial Executives Institute, the Institute of Management Accountants, the American Institute of Certified Public Accountants, the New York State Society of Certified Public Accountants, and the Illinois State Society of Certified Public Accountants. She has held various national positions with these organizations, including Chairman of FEI. She also serves on the Board of the Council for Ethics in Economics.

Nathan T. Garrett, 1989–1991.

Nate Garrett was nominated for the AECC by the National Association of State Boards of Accountancy. He chaired the Regulatory Issues and Professional Examinations Task Forces. He was liaison to the North Carolina A & T grant project.

Mr. Garrett is a partner with Garrett and Davenport, CPAs, P.C. and Assistant Professor of Accounting and Law at North Carolina Central University. He was a member of the Board of Trustees of Duke University and was Chairman of the first United Negro College Fund drive in the Research Triangle communities. He received the Outstanding Achievements award from the National Association of Black Accountants and was President of the National Association of Minority CPA Firms.

Mr. Garrett was a member of the North Carolina Board of CPA Examiners and is a Past Chairman of the National Association of State Boards of Accountancy. He served on the Editorial Review Committee of the *Journal of Accountancy*.

A graduate of Yale University, Mr. Garrett received his J.D. from the North Carolina Central University of Law.

Barron H. Harvey, 1994–1996.

Barron Harvey served on the Student Recruiting and Assessment Task Forces.

Dr. Harvey is a Professor of Accounting and Dean of the School of Business at Howard University. He holds M.B.A. and Ph.D. degrees from the University of Nebraska and is a Certified Public Accountant in the state of Maryland and the District of Columbia. Dr. Harvey has held academic and professional appointments at several institutions including the University of Nebraska, the University of Miami, Georgetown University, and Howard University. He has received numerous awards and honors, including the Richard D. Irwin/Beta Gamma Sigma Faculty Fellow for Teaching Excellence; Outstanding Accounting Leader, National Association of Black Accountants, Metro Washington, D.C. Chapter; The Regents Fellowship Award; Howard University School of Business Outstanding Faculty Award; and AACSB Fellow.

Dr. Harvey is a member of many academic and professional organizations including: Executive Committee on Education; American Institute of Certified Public Accountants; Board of Directors, Washington Campus Schools; Chairperson, Curriculum and Instruction Committee, American Institute of Certified Public Accountants; Co-chairperson, Pre-Licensing Education Advisory Committee, District of Columbia Board of Accountancy; Research Committee, Graduate Management Admissions Council; American Accounting Association; D.C. Institute of Schools Business Research Forum; 1992 Program Director, Nissan Summer Faculty Development Seminar; and National Association of Black Accountants. In addition, Dr. Harvey is the founder of the Washington Consortium Schools of Business Research Forum.

Professor Harvey has published in *Spectrum* and *Internal Auditing*. He has devoted his career to increasing business and accounting educational opportunities for disadvantaged students.

Charles T. Horngren, 1989–1992.

Charles Horngren chaired the Instructional Materials Task Force and was a member of the Faculty Development Task Force.

Dr. Horngren was the Edmund W. Littlefield Professor of Accounting at Stanford University while serving on the AECC; he is currently Professor Emeritus. A graduate of Marquette University, he received his M.B.A. from Harvard University and his Ph.D. from the University of Chicago. He is also the recipient of honorary doctorates from Marquette University and DePaul University.

A Certified Public Accountant, Professor Horngren served on the Accounting Principles Board for six years, the Financial Accounting Standards Board Advisory Council for five years, and the Council of the American Institute of Certified Public Accountants for three years. For six years, he served as a trustee of the Financial Accounting Foundation, which oversees the Financial Accounting Standards Board and the Government Accounting Standards Board.

Professor Horngren is a member of the Accounting Hall of Fame. He has received outstanding educator awards from the American Accounting Association, the American Institute of Certified

Public Accountants, the California CPA Foundation, and the Institute of Management Accountants. He was President and Director of Research of the American Accounting Association and is the author of numerous books and articles.

Donald E. Kieso, 1989–1993.

Don Kieso was AECC liaison to the Kansas State University grant project. He also chaired the Faculty Incentives Task Force and was a member of the Professional Examinations Task Force.

Dr. Kieso was the KPMG Peat Marwick Professor at Northern Illinois University while serving on the AECC; he is now Professor Emeritus. He is a graduate of Aurora University (B.S.) and the University of Illinois (M.A.S., Ph. D., and CPA) and had done postdoctorate work at the University of California at Berkeley. He has public accounting experience at Price Waterhouse (San Francisco and Chicago) and Arthur Andersen (Chicago) and research experience in the Research Division of the AICPAs in New York.

Dr. Kieso has served as Secretary-Treasurer of both the American Accounting Association and the Federation of Schools of Accountancy and on numerous committees of those organizations. He has also served on the Board of Directors of the Illinois CPA Society, the AAA Administrators of Accounting Programs Group (now the Accounting Programs Leadership Group), and AACSB Accreditation and Standards Committees. He currently serves as Chairman of the Board of Trustees of Aurora University and Treasurer of the Board of Directors of Sandwich Community Hospital, and is on the Boards of Directors of Castle BancGroup, Inc. and the Sandwich State Bank.

Dr. Kieso has received several teaching awards, including the NIU Teaching Excellence Award and four Golden Apple Awards, and in 1988 was named the Outstanding Educator of the Year by the Illinois CPA Society. In 1992 he received the FSA's Joseph A. Silvoso Award of Merit and the NIU Foundation's Humanitarian Award for Service to Higher Education. In 1995 he received a Distinguished Service Award from the Illinois CPA Society. He is the author of numerous publications, including eight books on business and accounting topics.

David L. Landsittel, 1992–1996.

David Landsittel was the AECC liaison to both Kirkwood Community College and University of Chicago grant projects. He chaired the Assessment Task Force and was a member of the Professional Examination Task Force.

Mr. Landsittel, a CPA, was an audit partner with the firm of Arthur Andersen & Co. until his retirement in 1997. He served as Managing Director of Auditing Procedures and Director of SEC Policies for the firm. Mr. Landsittel is a member of the American Institute of Certified Public Accountants and has served as chairman of its Auditing Standards Board and as a member of AICPA Council. He chaired the Institute's task force charged with addressing the auditor's responsibility for fraud detection. He has also served on the Advisory Council for the Committee on Sponsoring Organizations charged with developing integrated guidance in internal control in response to a Treadway Commission recommendation. He recently received from the Public Oversight Board the John J. McCloy Award for outstanding contributions to auditing in the United States.

Mr. Landsittel is active in the Illinois CPA Society and has served as its President. He is also a member of the American Accounting Association, has published articles dealing with accounting and auditing, and has served on the editorial boards for several professional journals. Prior to joining Arthur Andersen & Co., Mr. Landsittel received an M.B.A. from the University of Chicago Graduate School of Business and an undergraduate degree from DePauw University in Indiana.

Rev. Paul L. Locatelli, S.J., 1989–1996.

Paul Locatelli was a member of the Commission for its entire life. He served on the Leadership Support and Assessment Task Forces and was Project Director and co-author of the AECC monograph, *Assessment for the New Curriculum: A Guide for Professional Accounting Programs.*

Rev. Locatelli is the President of Santa Clara University. He has a bachelor's degree in accounting from Santa Clara University, a doctorate of business administration with an emphasis in accounting from the University of Southern California, and a master of divinity from the Jesuit School of Theology in Berkeley. He entered the Jesuit Order in 1962 and became a CPA in 1965. In 1974, he joined the accounting faculty at Santa Clara University, served as Associate Dean for the business school and Academic Vice President.

He has served as vice-chair of the Association of Jesuit Colleges and Universities and on the Board of Trustees at Regis University, Boards of Directors of the American Leadership Forum Joint Venture: Silicon Valley and its 21st Century Education Initiative, the National Conference of Christians and Jews, Board of Governors of the Institute of European and Asian Studies, and the Executive Committee of the Association of Independent California Colleges and Universities. He has also served on Boards of Trustees for four universities and on the Senior Accrediting Commission of Western Association of Schools and Colleges (WASC) as well as its Board of Directors.

Dr. Locatelli is a member of the American Institute of Certified Public Accountants, American Accounting Association, and the California Society of Certified Public Accountants.

James K. Loebbecke, 1989–1992.

Jim Loebbecke chaired the Objectives of Education for Accountants and Measurement of Educational Change Task Forces.

Professor Loebbecke is the Kenneth A. Sorensen KPMG Peat Marwick Professor of Accounting at the University of Utah. As of July 1, 1999 he will be Professor Emeritus. Professor Loebbecke is widely known for his research and writing in the auditing area. Among his many auditing publications are *Auditing: An Integrated Approach* and *Applications of Statistical Sampling to Auditing*, both co-authored with Alvin A. Arens.

Professor Loebbecke is very active in professional organizations, including the AICPA and the American Accounting Association, where he has held various positions. He was the academic member of the Auditing Standards Board from 1984 through 1987, and during 1982–1983 he was the Chairman of the Auditing Section of the American Accounting Association. Prior to 1980, Professor Loebbecke was a partner with Touche Ross & Company, where he was National Director of Auditing Standards from 1973–1978.

Gerhard G. Mueller, 1992–1996.

Gerry Mueller was Chairman of the AECC, 1994–1996. He was the AECC liaison for the Arizona State University grant project and chaired the Curriculum Dissemination Task Force.

Dr. Mueller was the Julius A. Roller Professor of Accounting at the University of Washington and is currently a member of the Financial Accounting Standards Board. His prior service at the University of Washington includes Acting Dean, Senior Associate Dean, Chair of the Department of Accounting, and Director of the Master of Professional Accounting program. He received B.S., B.B.A., and Ph.D. degrees from the University of California at Berkeley, and is a CPA with wide business and government experience. During 1988–1989 he served as President of both the American Accounting Association and the Washington Society of CPAs. He is past chairman of the Board of Trustees of Overlake Hospital Medical Center in Bellevue, Washington.

Dr. Mueller has lectured at numerous universities, conferences, and management programs in both the United States and abroad. He is the author, co-author or co-editor of 19 books and more than 100 professional journal articles and reviews. His biographical listings appear in *Who's Who in the World* and *Who's Who in America*, among others. He serves on several national advisory committees and boards of directors. He is a fellow of the Academy of International Business. He has received several distinguished teaching awards and three outstanding educator awards (American Accounting Association, 1982; Washington Society of CPAs, 1985; Beta Alpha Psi, 1987). He received the Wildman Medal Award in 1986. During 1987, he served as the American Accounting Association Distinguished International Visiting Lecturer in seven African countries.

James Naus, 1993–1996.

Jim Naus was a member of the Professional Examinations Task Force and the VIP Contacts Project Team.

Mr. Naus received his B.S. in business from Miami University and his M.A.S. in Accounting from the University of Illinois. He is currently Managing Partner of Crowe Chizek and Company LLP.

Mr. Naus is a member of the American Institute of Certified Public Accountants and the Indiana CPA Society. He is a former Chairman, Board of Examiners, AICPA; a former Board member and a former member of the Accounting Theory Subcommittee. He has served on the AICPA Ethics Executive Committee and the Technical Standards Subcommittee. Mr. Naus is a past president and former trustee of the Indiana CPA Education Foundation. Mr. Naus has published several articles in professional journals.

Melvin C. O'Connor, 1989–1996.

Mel O'Connor was a member of the Commission for its entire life. He was the liaison to the joint grant project at the Universities of Illinois and Notre Dame, and he chaired the Accreditation Task Force and the Dissemination Conferences Project Team. He was also a member of the Leadership Support, Faculty Development, and Faculty Incentives Task Forces and the Learning to Learn Project Team.

Dr. O'Connor is the Deloitte & Touche Professor of Accounting, former Chairperson of the Department of Accounting, former Director of the Accounting Doctoral Program, and former Director of the Program in professional Accounting at Michigan State University. He has bachelor's, master's, and Ph.D. degrees from the University of Kansas. Dr. O'Connor is a member of the American Institute of Certified Public Accountants, the Michigan Association of Certified Public Accountants, and the American Accounting Association. He is a past president of the AAA Administrators of Accounting Programs Group (now the Accounting Programs Leadership Group) and a former member of the AAA Council. He served for several years as a member of the Accounting Accreditation and Visitation Committees of the American Assembly of Collegiate Schools of Business. Dr. O'Connor was on the editorial board of *Issues in Accounting Education* and is an author or co-author of numerous articles, monographs, and books.

Vincent M. O'Reilly, 1989–1992.

Vin O'Reilly chaired the Change Commission Progress and University Support Task Forces and was a member of the Early Employment Experience Task Force.

Before retiring in 1998, Mr. O'Reilly was Executive Vice Chairman of Coopers & Lybrand LLP and served on the Firm's Management Committee and on its predecessor Executive Committee. Prior to becoming Executive Vice Chairman, Mr. O'Reilly was Chief Operating Officer of the Firm and the founding Chairman of the International Accounting and Auditing Services Group.

Mr. O'Reilly joined Coopers & Lybrand in 1991. He was the Managing Partner of the Boston Office from 1980 to 1983. From 1983 to 1988 he was the Regional Managing Partner of the Firm's Northeast Region, which includes offices in New England and upstate New York.

Mr. O'Reilly is a member of the SEC Practice Section Executive Committee of the American Institute of Certified Public Accountants. He was also a member of the Financial Accounting Standards Advisory Council of the Financial Accounting Foundation. He is a member of the Board of Directors of The Neiman Marcus Group and was also selected as a Director of the newly formed New England Independent System Operator. He was the editor of *Montgomery's Auditing* and authored *Internal Control-Integrated Framework*.

Mr. O'Reilly is active in numerous community and not-for-profit organizations. He was Chairman and remains Vice Chairman of the Board of the Dana-Farber Cancer Institute, which is the regional cancer facility for New England and a leading research institution. In addition, he is a Trustee of the Boston Symphony Orchestra and a member of the National Development Board of Boston College.

Mr. O'Reilly is a graduate of Boston College and received an M.B.A. from the Wharton School of Finance at the University of Pennsylvania.

David B. Pearson, 1994–1996.

Dave Pearson was nominated for the Commission by the Sponsors' Task Force. He was on the CPA Examinations Task Force.

Dr. Pearson was the National Director of Audit Quality Control for Ernst & Young LLP during his tenure on the Commission. After the merger of Ernst & Whinney and Arthur Young, he was involved in developing, implementing and monitoring the firm's audit and quality control policies and procedures. From 1973 to 1979 he was one of the predecessor firm's Director of Continuing Professional Education.

Dr. Pearson has served on numerous committees of the AICPA concerned with university and continuing education, the CPA examination, and auditing and quality control, including the Auditing Standards Board and the Peer Review Committee of the SEC Practice Section, including three years (1986–1989) as Chairman. He also served on the AICPA Council as a member-at-large. He has also been a member of the Board of Examiners and its Auditing and Standards Setting Subcommittees. He currently is the Chairman of the Board of Examiners and a member of the Quality Control Inquiry Committee.

Dr. Pearson has been a Vice President of the American Accounting Association and the Secretary-Treasurer of the American Assembly of Collegiate Schools of Business (AACSB), and was a member of the AACSB Peer Review Improvement Task Force. He has been involved in accreditation activities since the mid-1970s.

In 1996 he received the Public Oversight Board's John J. McCloy Award for outstanding contributions to audit excellence. Currently, he is the Director of the Board's Blue Ribbon Panel on Audit Effectiveness.

Dr. Pearson received his master's and doctorate degrees from Indiana University and received the national gold medal award on the November 1960 CPA examination. He has taught at Indiana and Columbia Universities. He is now on the faculty of Case Western Reserve University.

Stanley R. Pylipow, 1993–1996.

Stan Pylipow was nominated for the AECC by the Institute of Management of Accountants. He was liaison to the Kansas State University grant project, and he was a member of the Curriculum Dissemination Task Force and the Dissemination Conferences Project Team.

Mr. Pylipow is in his second career, assisting the management of closely held businesses in assessing, developing, evaluating, and implementing business plans. He also serves as an outside director on the Boards of an engineering and architectural consulting firm and a publishing company.

Mr. Pylipow concluded a 35-year corporate career as Vice President and Chief Financial Officer of Fisher Controls International, Inc. Following receipt of a B.B.A. in Accounting from St. Bonaventure University in 1957, he joined Chicopee Manufacturing, the textile subsidiary of Johnson and Johnson. In 1965 he joined Mobil Chemical, in 1974 moved to Monsanto and then on to the Fisher subsidiary in 1979.

Long active in the Institute of Management Accountants (formerly NAA), he served as National President in 1990–1991. He is also a member of the Financial Executives. He is a past member of the Finance Council of the Manufacturer's Alliance for Productivity Improvement and the Institute of Management Consultants.

Active in his community, he is a Past President of the Ecumenical Housing Production Corporation and has been honored by Professional Secretaries International as Executive of the Year and as a recipient of the Monsanto Volunteer Excellence Award.

R. Eugene Rice, 1994–1996.

Dr. Rice is Scholar in Residence and Director of the Forum on Faculty Roles and Rewards at the American Association for Higher Education, Washington, D.C. Before moving to AAHE, he was Vice President and Dean of the Faculty at Antioch College, where he held a tenured appointment as Professor of Sociology and Religion. Previous to his work at Antioch, Dr. Rice was Senior Fellow at the Carnegie Foundation engaged in the national study of the scholarly priorities of the American professoriate and collaborating with the late Ernest Boyer on the Carnegie Report, *Scholarship Reconsidered*.

During the major part of his career, Dr. Rice was Professor of Sociology and Religion at the University of the Pacific, where he helped initiate the first of the experimental "cluster colleges" and served as Chairperson of the Department of Sociology. His teaching and research focus on the sociology and ethics of the professions and the workplace. He received his Ph.D. from Harvard University and is a graduate of the Harvard Divinity School and Pasadena College.

In addition to directing the Forum on Faculty Roles and Rewards at AAHE, Dr. Rice also provides leadership for the New Pathways project "Academic Careers for a New Century: From Inquiry to Practice." Gene is the recipient of the Academic Leadership Award (for exemplary contributions to American higher education) given by the Council of Independent Colleges, and received the Mina Shaughnessy Scholars Award from the Fund for the Improvement of Post-Secondary Education. He has served on the board of directors of the Society for Values in Higher Education and the national advisory committee of the Preparing Future Faculty project sponsored by the Pew Charitable Trusts.

In *Change* magazine's 1998 survey of America's higher education leaders, Dr. Rice is recognized as one of a small group of "idea leaders" whose work has made a national difference.

Katherine Schipper, 1991–1996.

Katherine Schipper chaired the Faculty Development Task Force and was a member of the Learning to Learn Project Team.

Dr. Schipper is the Eli B. and Harriet B. Williams Professor of Accounting and KPMG Peat Marwick Faculty Research Scholar at the University of Chicago Graduate School of Business. She received both M.B.A. and Ph.D. degrees, as well as an M.A. in Library Science, from the University of Chicago. After completing her graduate work at Chicago and prior to joining the Chicago faculty in 1983, she was a member of the faculty of the Graduate School of Industrial Administration at Carnegie Mellon University for seven years.

Dr. Schipper is a member of the American Accounting Association, and has served as its President and Director of Research. She has published numerous research papers on various aspects of corporate restructuring and financial reporting. She has served as the editor of the *Journal of Accounting Research* and has served as an editorial board member for several accounting journals.

William Shenkir, 1991–1996.

Bill Shenkir served as Vice-Chair of the Commission, 1991–1994. He was the AECC liaison to the North Carolina A & T grant project, chaired the Ad Hoc Articulation Task Force, and was a member of the Assessment Task Force.

Dr. Shenkir is the William Stamps Farish Professor of Free Enterprise at the McIntire School of Commerce, University of Virginia. He received a bachelor's degree in business administration from Texas A&M University and master's and doctoral degrees from the University of Texas. He studied at Drew University on a Rockefeller Brothers Theological Fellowship.

Professor Shenkir joined the McIntire School faculty in 1967. In 1973, he became a technical advisor to a member of the Financial Accounting Standards Board. Subsequently, he served as one of the Board's five project directors. He returned to the University of Virginia in 1977 as the Dean of the McIntire School of Commerce, a position he held until 1992.

Professor Shenkir served as president of the American Assembly of Collegiate Schools of Business during 1990–1991 and as vice president of the American Accounting Association during 1986–1988. He has also served a three-year term on the AICPA Council. He is a member of the Board of Directors of First Union National Bank of Virginia and is on the Board of ComSonics, Inc. He has published numerous articles in professional journals and edited or co-authored five books.

Ray M. Sommerfeld, 1989–1992.

The late Ray Sommerfeld chaired the Faculty Development Task Force and was a member of the University Support Task Force.

Dr. Sommerfeld held the James L. Bayless/Rauscher Pierce Refsnes, Inc. Chair in Business Administration at the Graduate School of Business, the University of Texas, where he was also a Professor of Accounting. Dr. Sommerfeld authored or co-authored eight books on taxation, including numerous editions of two innovative tax textbooks.

Dr. Sommerfeld was President of the American Accounting Association (AAA) and the American Taxation Association (ATA) as well as a former partner and National Director of Tax Education for Arthur Young & Co. (now Ernst & Young). Among other positions, Dr. Sommerfeld served on the IRS Commissioner's Advisory Committee, the FASB Task Force on Income Tax Allocation, and the Board of Directors for the Texas Society of CPAs (TSCPA). He was an active member of the AAA, ATA, TSCPA, and the AICPA and served as a consultant to various business and professional firms.

Joan S. Stark, 1989–1994.

Joan Stark was the AECC liaison to the Learning to Learn Project Team and a co-author of the resulting monograph, *Intentional Learning: A Process for Learning to Learn in the Accounting Curriculum*. She was also a member of the Faculty Development, Curriculum Dissemination, and Measurement of Educational Change Task Forces. Her extensive knowledge of the educational research literature and her ability to relate it to accounting education was invaluable to the Commission.

Dr. Stark is Professor of Higher Education at the University of Michigan and former editor of *The Review of Higher Education*, the journal of the Association for the Study of Higher Education, of which she is past national president. She was named a distinguished member of the Association for Institutional Research and received the Career Research Achievement Award and National Service Award from the Association for the Study of Higher Education and the Distinguished Research Award from Division J of the American Educational Research Association.

Professor Stark has been a college science instructor, a department chairperson, associate dean of a liberal arts college, and dean of the School of Education at the University of Michigan. She has written numerous articles and books on college course planning and curriculum development. She has co-authored such monographs as: *Strengthening the Ties that Bind: Integrating Undergraduate Liberal and Professional Study* (1988), *Responsive Professional Education: Balancing Outcomes and Opportunities* (1986), *Improving Teaching and Learning Through Research* (1988), and *Shaping the College Curriculum: Academic Plans in Action* (1997).

A. Marvin Strait, 1989–1993.

Marvin Strait was nominated for the AECC by the American Institute of Certified Public Accountants. He was AECC liaison to the Arizona State University grant project. He also chaired the Leadership Support Task Force and was a member of the Early Employment Experience Task Force.

Mr. Strait, CPA, received a Bachelor of Science Degree with Distinction from Arizona State University in 1957. He started his CPA practice in 1959 in Lamar, Colorado, where he was the only CPA in that five-county corner of the state. In 1973 he became a partner in Stone, Gray and Company, and in 1977, when Stone, Gray and Company merged with a major firm, Mr. Strait elected to continue as an independent, forming Strait Kushinsky and Company. In 1993 Strait Kushinsky and Company combined its operations with Baird, Kurtz & Dobson, where Mr. Strait served as a partner until 1994. He now practices public accountancy under the name of A. Marvin Strait, CPA.

Mr. Strait has served as President of the Colorado Society of Certified Public Accountants and the Colorado State Board of Accountancy. In 1987–1988, he was Chairman of the Board of Directors of the American Institute of Certified Public Accountants. In 1992 Mr. Strait was awarded the AICPA Gold Medal for Distinguished Service. He currently is a Member of the Board of Management for the AICPA Continuing Professional Education program and is a permanent member of the AICPA Governing Council.

Mr. Strait has served a Chairman of the Board of the Colorado Springs Chamber of Commerce, the St. Francis Hospital Board of Directors, the Colorado Springs Utilities Financial Advisory Board, and the Penrose-St. Francis Healthcare Audit Committee. He is currently the Treasurer and Chairman of the Finance committee for the Colorado Springs Fine Arts Center. He also is a member of the Board of Directors for Western National Bank and Colorado Technical University. Mr. Strait is also a member of the Audit Committee of the United States Olympic Committee.

Gary L. Sundem, 1989–1991.

Gary Sundem was Executive Director of the AECC, 1989–1991. He was a member of the Objectives of Education for Accountants, Information Dissemination, Grant Program, and Two-Year Schools Task Forces.

During his tenure as Executive Director of the Commission, Professor Sundem was on leave of absence from his faculty position at the University of Washington, where he is currently Julius A. Roller Professor of Accounting and Co-Chair of the Department of Accounting. He has held a variety of positions in the American Accounting Association, including President (1992–1993) and editor of *The Accounting Review* (1982–1986). He has also been active in the Institute of Management Accountants, including serving on the National Board of Directors and as President of the Seattle Chapter, and in the Financial Executives Institute.

Professor Sundem received his B.A. degree from Carleton College and his M.B.A. and Ph.D. degrees from Stanford University. He has received several awards, including the 1998 Outstanding Educator Award from the AAA, the 1987 Outstanding Accounting Educator Award from the Washington Society of CPAs, and the 1977 AICPA/AAA Notable Contribution to Accounting Literature Award. He is co-author of two textbooks and author of numerous journal articles. He serves on the Board of Rainier Investment Management Mutual Funds and has been on many civic and non-profit boards.

Richard R. West, 1989–1991.

Dick West was nominated for the AECC by the American Assembly of Collegiate Schools of Business. He was a member of the Faculty Incentives and Accreditation Task Forces.

Dr. West was Dean of the Leonard N. Stern School of Business at New York University at the time he served on the AECC. He has also been Dean of the Amos Tuck School of Business Administration at Dartmouth College and the College of Business of the University of Oregon. He currently serves on the boards of several major corporations and a number of mutual funds.

Dr. West is a graduate of Yale University (B.A.) and the University of Chicago (M.B.A. and Ph.D.). He has served as a trustee of the Joint Council on Economic Education and as Chair of the Municipal Securities Rule-Making Board and is a former member of the Board of Governors of the National Association of Securities Dealers. He is the author or co-author of three books and more than 50 articles about finance and financial markets.

Doyle Z. Williams, 1989–1993.

Doyle Williams was Chairman of the AECC, 1989–1993, and Executive Director, 1991–1993. He chaired the Grant Program Task Force and was a member of the Information Dissemination Task Force.

Dr. Williams was the founding Dean of the School of Accounting at the University of Southern California, where he served as the Peat Marwick Main Professor at USC. He is currently Sam M. Walton Leadership Chair and Dean of the College of Business at the University of Arkansas.

Dr. Williams has served in many leadership positions, including President of the American Accounting Association, President of the Federation of Schools of Accountancy, President of the Administrators of Accounting Programs Group (now the Accounting Programs Leadership Group), and Vice President and member of the Board of Directors and Council of the American Institute of Certified Public Accountants. He received Outstanding Accounting Educator Awards from the American Institute of Certified Public Accountants and the American Accounting Association. He also received the National Leadership Award from the Academy of Business Administration.

A graduate of Northwestern State University of Louisiana (B.S.) and Louisiana State University (M.S. and Ph.D.), Dr. Williams is the author of numerous articles and monographs and contributor to several books.

G. Peter Wilson, 1992–1996.

Pete Wilson was a member of the Faculty Development Task Force and the Learning to Learn Project Team. As a member of the AAA Education Advisory Committee, he was instrumental in transferring the AECC's faculty development thrust to the AAA upon the expiration of the Commission.

Dr. Wilson holds the Joseph L. Sweeney Chair of Accounting at Boston College. After receiving B.S. and M.S. degrees in mathematics from Florida Atlantic University in 1970, he taught at Lake Sumter Community College for eight years. In 1985 he received his Ph.D. from Carnegie Mellon University and joined the faculty at the Stanford Graduate School of Business. He served on the faculties of Harvard University and the Massachusetts Institute of Technology before joining the Boston College faculty in 1997.

Dr. Wilson received the American Accounting Association's Competitive Manuscript Award in 1986, the Distinguished Teaching Award at the Stanford Business School in 1988, and the Teacher of the Year Award at the Sloan School of Management at M.I.T. in 1995. He is a member of the American Accounting Association, where he served as Academic Vice President, and he is on the editorial boards of the *Journal of Accounting Research, The Financial Officer's Tax and Management Report*, and *Issues in Accounting Education*.

Dr. Wilson's research papers investigate the usefulness and reliability of accounting accruals and the ways in which tax status, changes in tax rules, and nontax business factors affect managers' investment, operating, financing, and reporting decisions. He teaches and develops teaching cases for courses closely related to his research interests, including analysis of corporate reports, taxes, and economic behavior.

Robert E. Witt, 1992–1996.

Bob Witt was nominated for the AECC by the American Assembly of Collegiate Schools of Business. He was a member of the Faculty Development Task Force.

During his time on the AECC, Dr. Witt served as Dean of the College and Graduate School of Business at the University of Texas at Austin 1986–1995. He is now President of the University of Texas at Arlington. He joined the Department of Marketing at the University of Texas at Austin in 1968 as an Assistant Professor and served as Department Chairman from 1973–1983. He served as Associate Dean for Academic Affairs from 1983–85 and Acting Dean from 1985–1986. He held the Centennial Chair in Business Education Leadership, the Betty and Glenn Mortimer Centennial Professorship in Business, and the Gale Centennial Professor in Business.

Dr. Witt received a bachelor's degree from Bates College, an M.B.A. from Dartmouth College, and a Ph.D. from Pennsylvania State University. He has served on the Board of Directors of the American Assembly of Collegiate Schools of Business (AACSB), as well as on a number of AACSB committees. He serves on the Graduate Management Admission Council (GMAC) Board and has served as a director of several corporations.

EX OFFICIO:

Michael A. Diamond, 1995–1996.

Mike Diamond represented the American Accounting Association as its Director of Education. Because he was the AAA Director of Education at the end of the AECC's life, Mike was largely responsible for the transfer of activities from the Commission to the AAA.

Dr. Diamond is Executive Vice Provost of the University of Southern California, where he has also served as Dean of the Levanthal School of Accounting, Director of the School's SEC and Financial Reporting Institute, and Vice Provost for Planning and Budget. Prior to becoming Dean at USC, Professor Diamond taught at California State University, Los Angeles. He holds a Ph.D. and an M.S. in Accounting from UCLA and a B.A. in History from the University of California at Berkeley.

Dr. Diamond is the 1998–1999 President of the American Accounting Association, where he has served as President of the Administrators of Accounting Programs Group (now the Accounting Programs Leadership Group) and Chair of the New Faculty Consortium Committee, as well as Director of Education. He has written two accounting textbooks, as well as published articles in *Accounting Horizons*, *Journal of Accountancy*, and *Harvard Business Review*. He is active in the AICPA and the California Society of CPAs. He received the California Society of CPAs Faculty Excellence Award in 1993. He also consults with The Strategic Planning Partnership, an initiative of the Ernst & Young Foundation, which assists selected business schools and other academic organizations in strategic planning and change-management processes.

Rick Elam, 1989–1995.

Rick Elam represented the American Institute of Certified Public Accountants as its Vice President, Education. He was a member of the Regulatory Issues, Professional Examinations, Faculty Development, Student Recruiting, and Curriculum Dissemination Task Forces.

Before joining the AICPA, Dr. Elam was Dean of the School of Business at Rutgers University–Camden, and before that he was Director of the School of Accountancy at the University of Missouri–Columbia. He is currently Dean of the College of Business at Middle Tennessee State University.

Dr. Elam holds a B.S. degree from Culver-Stockton College and M.A. and Ph.D. degrees from the University of Missouri–Columbia. He is a past-president of the Federation of Schools of

Accountancy and has been on the Accreditation Committee of the AACSB. He has been on numerous professional and civic boards, including the Missouri Society of CPAs, the Camden County Private Industry Council and the Chamber of Commerce of Southern New Jersey. He is the author of numerous articles.

Robert W. Ingram, 1991–1993.

Rob Ingram represented the American Accounting Association as its Director of Education. He was on the Two-Year Schools Task Force and the Screening Committee for Grants to Two-Year Schools.

Currently the Ross-Culverhouse Endowed Chair of Accountancy and Director, S. Paul Garner Center for Current Accounting Issues at the University of Alabama, Dr. Ingram was Ernst & Young Professor and Director of the Culverhouse School of Accountancy at Alabama during his time on the Commission. He served as editor of *Issues in Accounting Education* from 1985–1988.

Dr. Ingram received his B.A. degree at Eastern New Mexico University, his M.A. at Abilene Christian University, and his Ph.D. at Texas Tech University. Dr. Ingram has published several research monographs and books. His articles have appeared in *Journal of Accounting Research*, *The Accounting Review*, *Journal of Finance*, and *Journal of Accounting and Public Policy*, among others. He is a CPA.

Corine T. Norgaard, 1989–1991.

Corine Norgaard represented the American Accounting Association as its Director of Education. She chaired the Two-Year Schools Task Force and was a member of the Faculty Development Task Force.

While on the Commission, Dr. Norgaard was Professor of Accounting and Director of Executive Programs at the University of Connecticut. After her service on the AECC, she became Dean of the School of Management at SUNY at Binghamton and is currently Dean of the Barney School of Business and Public Administration at the University of Hartford. She chairs the Audit Committees for Advest, Aetna Variable Fund, Aetna Encore Fund, and Aetna Income Shares.

Dr. Norgaard received her B.B.A. and M.B.A. degrees from North Texas State University and her Ph.D. from the University of Texas at Austin. She is a textbook author and has published numerous articles in academic and professional journals.

Jan R. Williams, 1993–1995.

Jan Williams represented the American Accounting Association as its Director of Education. He was a member of the Faculty Development and Ad Hoc Articulation Task Forces.

Dr. Williams is the Ernst & Young Professor and Associate Dean for Academic Programs, College of Business Administration, University of Tennessee, Knoxville. He received his B.S. degree from George Peabody College, his M.B.A. from Baylor University, and his Ph.D. from the University of Arkansas. He is a CPA in Arkansas and Tennessee.

Dr. Williams served as Director of Education of the American Accounting Association. He is co-author of AAA Accounting Education Research Monograph #9, *Framework for the Development of Accounting Education Research*. He has served as President of the Administrators of Accounting Programs Group (now the Accounting Programs Leadership Group) of the AAA, Chair of the Teaching and Curriculum Section, and Vice President of the Southeast Region. He was elected President-elect of the AAA in August 1998, and will serve as the organization's President in 1999–2000.

He is actively involved in several professional organizations other than the AAA, including the AICPA, the Tennessee Society of CPAs, and the Federation of Schools of Accountancy. He served as National President of Beta Alpha Psi in 1987–1988 and was on leave from his university during 1991–1992, serving as an educational consultant in Ernst & Young's national office. He received the AICPA's Outstanding Accounting Educator Award for 1994.

APPENDIX B

Perspectives on Education: Capabilities for Success in the Accounting Profession

Big 8 White Paper

FOREWORD

We have developed this paper because of our concerns regarding the quality and number of accounting graduates available to the public accounting profession. At the same time, questions are being raised by the academic community regarding the effectiveness of accounting education. We believe our views are supportive of previous efforts by the American Accounting Association (AAA) and the American Institute of Certified Public Accountants (AICPA). We particularly applaud the AAA's Committee on the Future Structure, Content, and Scope of Accounting Education (the Bedford Committee) and its follow-up groups. The analysis and recommendations by that committee provide an excellent foundation for the future of accounting education, including curriculum content, the teaching process and faculty responsibilities.

In this paper, our focus is not on specific course content or the number of hours in the curriculum, but on the capabilities needed by the profession that should be developed through the educational process. We recognize that the role of the profession is to specify and communicate the skills and knowledge needed to be an accomplished practitioner. Responsibility for curriculum development and appropriate teaching methods rests primarily with the academic community. However, we believe any successful effort to enhance education for accounting will be achieved only through a partnership of faculty and practitioners.

As part of our contribution to this coordinated effort, we are prepared to make a five-year commitment of up to $4 million to support the development of stimulating and relevant curricula. The major portion of these resources is for grants to colleges and universities to support the development of curricula that are responsive to the needs of the profession. The commitment of these funds is contingent on the condition that they be used effectively and in a timely way for the design and implementation of innovative curricula, new teaching methods and supporting materials that will equip graduates with the capabilities for success in our profession.

Our firms look forward to the opportunity to participate in a coordinated approach by the major professional and academic groups to shape the future direction of education for the accounting profession.

Duane R. Kullberg
Arthur Andersen & Co.

William L. Gladstone
Arthur Young

Peter R. Scanlon
Coopers & Lybrand

J. Michael Cook
Deloitte Haskins & Sells

April, 1989

Ray J. Groves
Ernst & Whinney

Larry D. Horner
Peat Marwick Main & Co.

Shaun F. O'Malley
Price Waterhouse

Edward A. Kangas
Touche Ross

CONTENTS

- The Current Environment

- Recommendation for Change

- The Capabilities Necessary for Practice

- Sources of Capabilities

- The Challenges for Education

- The Opportunity

THE CURRENT ENVIRONMENT

The accounting profession faces a unique convergence of forces, which creates a critical need to re-examine the educational process.

- The profession is changing, expanding and, as a result, becoming increasingly complex.
- Declining enrollments in accounting programs indicate that the profession is becoming less attractive to students.
- Implementation of the AICPA requirement of 150 hours of education for membership by the year 2000 must be addressed.

Today's business world is more dynamic and complex than ever before. Advancing technology, proliferating regulations, globalization of commerce and complex transactions make the environment in which public accountants practice extremely challenging. Successful practitioners must develop and apply a wide range of professional capabilities to serve the business community.

Many accounting programs have experienced declines in enrollments, and questions are being raised regarding the quality of accounting graduates. While the number of freshmen enrolling in business schools has grown substantially, the proportion of students planning to major in accounting has decreased. This decline in the attractiveness of accounting as a major may not be a significant issue if the resulting pool of graduates exhibits exceptional quality. However, there is some evidence that this may not be the situation, based on indicators such as scores on college entrance examinations.

The supply and demand imbalance is a very real problem for the profession. Over the last 10 years, demand from public accounting rose substantially, while there was only a slight increase in the supply of accounting graduates from institutions accredited by the American Assembly of Collegiate Schools of Business (AACSB).

The result is a decreasing ability to be selective in the recruiting process, which adversely affects the quality of new hires brought into the profession.

Also, the effectiveness of accounting programs is being questioned. The AAA's Bedford Committee undertook a comprehensive review of the subject. It found that while the profession has changed in recent years, accounting education has not and, as a result, "accounting education as it is currently approached requires major re-orientation between now and the year 2000."[*]

Extending university education for accounting majors has been under discussion for 20 years. As previously mentioned, the AICPA will require 150 hours of education for membership by the year 2000. Although the AICPA has provided guidance about the composition of the accounting curriculum in meeting this requirement, there is no apparent consensus among accounting educators regarding their support for these guidelines—or of alternative approaches. This issue must be addressed in the next several years, since students enrolling in college in the mid-1990s will need to meet this requirement. Effective marketing of this additional investment required of students will be essential to meet the demands of the profession.

RECOMMENDATIONS FOR CHANGE

The current environment makes real curricular change essential and necessitates response from a dynamic partnership between practitioners and academicians. First, the profession must specify the

---

[*] "Future Accounting Education: Preparing for the Expanding Profession," Special Report of the American Accounting Association Committee on the Future Structure, Content, and Scope of Accounting Education published in *Issues in Accounting Education*, 1986.

capabilities necessary for practice and communicate these to the academic community. With this input, faculty can develop a relevant and stimulating curriculum with state-of-the-art teaching methods.

Recognizing our responsibility to the profession, we have joined together to provide our views on the skills and knowledge needed by tomorrow's practitioner. Considering the diversity of practices in our firms, we believe that the capabilities outlined later in this paper are representative of the requirements for the profession. We also present the following recommendations for a coordinated approach to making changes in education for accounting:

- "The Capabilities Necessary for Practice," which follows these recommendations, should be used by the academic community as a statement of needs for the profession.
- A Coordinating committee of all major constituencies should be formed to address issues that impact the educational process and to guide the academic community in re-engineering the curriculum. Representation would include, among others, the AICPA, AAA, AACSB, National Association of State Boards of Accountancy (NASBA), Financial Executives Institute (FEI), National Association of Accountants (NAA) and the major firms.
- Our firms should participate in, and support, the coordinating committee and other appropriate groups with leadership, guidance and financial resources.
- The American Accounting Association, as the primary organization representing accounting faculty, should be encouraged to take the leadership role in establishing the coordinating committee. Efforts by the AAA to bring about the required curricular changes should be supported by the profession.
- Designated representatives from the profession should actively participate in the review of the accreditation standards to be conducted by the AACSB.

We also understand that external factors, such as professional examinations and conditions of licensure, affect the educational process. In the future, organizations responsible for such activities should recognize, in their policies and procedures, the broad skills and knowledge needed by the profession. Particularly important are the scope and timing of the CPA examinations.

THE CAPABILITIES NECESSARY FOR PRACTICE

The dialogue about education must be based on a clear statement of the capabilities needed for practice. Also, there must be a focus on the broader skills that will support a lifetime of professional success. Without a clear set of capabilities to use as objectives in the curriculum design process, it is unlikely that changes in the current content or teaching methods will be responsive to the needs of the profession.

In 1988, the AICPA issued a revised version of its *Education Requirements for Entry into the Accounting Profession*. That monograph includes an illustrative program of study with narrative descriptions of the appropriate content in specific areas. While the AICPA report and the capabilities described in this paper have much in common, the following focuses on the desired outcomes of the educational process, as contrasted with courses of study.

Education for the accounting profession must produce graduates who have a broad array of skills and knowledge.
Skills for Public Accounting
To be successful, an individual must bring to the practice several general skills. These are divided into three categories:

- Communication skills
- Intellectual skills
- Interpersonal skills

The categories are not mutually exclusive and cannot be considered in a vacuum. Obviously the communications skills are highly interrelated with the interpersonal skills, and some of the intellectual skills are dependent on some of the communication skills. The curriculum must support all of these skills.

Communication Skills
Public accounting requires its practitioners to be able to transfer and receive information with ease.

Practitioners must be able to present and defend their views through formal and informal, written and oral, presentation. They must be able to do so at a peer level with business executives.

As the rate of change in the business world increases, so does the amount of information that must be gathered from outside sources. Practitioners must be able to listen effectively to gain information and understand opposing points of view. They also will need the ability to locate, obtain and organize information from both human and electronic sources.

Intellectual Skills
Individuals seeking to be successful in the diverse world of public accounting must be able to use creative problem-solving skills in a consultative process. They must be able to solve diverse and unstructured problems in unfamiliar settings. They must be able to comprehend an unfocused set of facts; identify and, if possible, anticipate problems; and find acceptable solutions. This requires an understanding of the determining forces in a given situation and the ability to predict their effects.

Inductive thought processes and capabilities for judgment must be developed to support such activities. Practitioners must also be able to identify ethical issues and apply a value-based reasoning system to ethical questions.

The practice of public accounting, like the practice of any profession, includes many challenging pressures. Conflicting demands, unexpected requirements and coinciding deadlines are but a few of the sources of stress found in practice. The effective practitioner must be able to manage these pressures. This requires the ability and judgment to select and assign priorities within restricted resources and organize work to meet tight deadlines when necessary.

Interpersonal Skills
The ability to work with other human beings is an important part of public practice. Working effectively in groups with diverse members to accomplish a task is essential.

The practitioner must be able to influence others; organize and delegate tasks; motivate and develop other people; and withstand and resolve conflict. These are the skills of a competent manager. Because public accountants advise clients on the operation of their businesses, they should possess the requisite management skills. They must also be able to assume leadership positions within their own firms.

Knowledge for Public Accounting
An individual must also bring to the practice of public accounting a large body of knowledge. It is categorized here into three areas:
- General knowledge
- Organizational and business knowledge
- Accounting and auditing knowledge

To counter the temptation to focus only on knowledge directly related to accounting and auditing, this discussion starts with the general knowledge category.

General Knowledge

For the good of the profession and society as a whole, education for accounting must include a sufficiently large, broad and deep general education component to yield a level of knowledge that is characteristic of a broadly educated person.

The successful practitioner requires general knowledge that covers a number of factors:

- An understanding of the flow of events in history and the different cultures in today's world.
- The ability to interact with diverse groups of people and at the highest levels of intellectual exchange.
- A sense of the breadth of ideas, issues and contrasting economic, political and social forces in the world.
- Experience in making value judgments.

The general education component of university education should support the development of these factors and should leave the student excited about, and prepared for, lifelong learning.

Organizational and Business Knowledge

To understand their clients' and their own work environments, public accountants must have an understanding of the economic, social, cultural and psychological forces that affect organizations. They must also understand the basic internal workings of organizations and be able to apply this knowledge to specific examples. This requires an understanding of interpersonal and group dynamics.

Given the rapid pace of change in the business world, public accountants must understand the methods for creating and managing change in organizations. The professional environment is also characterized by rapidly increasing dependence on technological support. No understanding of organizations could be complete without attention to the current and future roles of information technology in client organizations and accounting practice.

Accounting and Auditing Knowledge

Post-secondary education should provide a strong fundamental understanding of accounting and auditing. This includes the history of the accounting profession and accounting thought, as well as the content, concepts, structure and meaning of reporting for organizational operations both for internal and external use. A companion area includes the methods for gathering, summarizing and analyzing financial data. Entering practitioners must also understand the meaning and application of, as well as the methodology for, attest services.

Accounting knowledge cannot focus solely on the construction of data. The ability to apply decision rules embodied in the accounting model is only a part of the goal. Accountants must be able to use the data, exercise judgments, evaluate risks and solve real-world problems.

Passing the CPA examination should not be the goal of accounting education. The focus should be on developing analytical and conceptual thinking—versus memorizing rapidly expanding professional standards.

SOURCES OF CAPABILITIES

The skills and knowledge that support the successful practitioner come from three sources:

- Talents
- Pre-entry education
- Continuing education and development

In this discussion, the term "pre-entry" is used to describe any education required prior to beginning licensing procedures. Under the present model, this may include both undergraduate and graduate education. The term "continuing education and development" includes all training, education and development during the period a person is involved in the public accounting profession. This encompasses all formal and informal, classroom and on-the-job, firm-supported or individual experiences.

Talents
Clearly, pre-entry education cannot bear the total responsibility for developing the capabilities discussed earlier. Each individual has inherent talents that will contribute to a successful professional career.

Pre-entry education must be perceived as sufficiently stimulating, interesting and rewarding to draw the best students. At the same time, the opportunities for challenging work, rewards and advancement in the public accounting profession must also be competitive to maintain a pool of high-talent practitioners.

Pre-Entry Education
Pre-entry education has focused on developing rule-based knowledge. Beyond anecdotal evidence, little is known about its ability to create or strengthen the other capabilities discussed in this paper. It seems to be a reasonable and necessary goal for pre-entry education to make significant improvements in these capabilities.

Continuing Education and Development
Major accounting firms devote significant resources to the continuing education and development of their personnel. These programs are an integral part of lifelong education for service in the public accounting profession. Any comprehensive effort to improve education for accounting must include continuing education and development. Challenging opportunities for learning and using skills and knowledge are an important part of the exciting and rewarding career that will attract and keep high-quality entrants.

Continuing education in the firms must meet several goals. First, it must support and enhance the knowledge and skills cited earlier. By doing so, it will achieve its second goal—to help attract and keep the best people in the profession.

To meet these goals, continuing education and development will require considerable commitment by the firms. As university curricula are re-engineered, continuing education must be redesigned. The focus on developing capabilities that is proposed for pre-entry education should become the model for education in practice. To support this comprehensive approach, licensing laws must include appropriate credit for continuing education in the development of all the capabilities. Restriction of full Continuing Professional Education credit to a narrow range of technical subjects would obstruct the development of the broad range of capabilities needed for the practice.

THE CHALLENGES FOR EDUCATION
To achieve pre-entry education that will develop the needed capabilities requires a complete re-engineering of the educational process. This includes defining objectives, content, design and methodology. Piecemeal responses to educational reforms will not suffice.

Major Components

Efforts to change education for accounting require consideration of five major components of higher education:

• Curriculum
• Faculty
• Students
• Universities
• Accreditation

Curriculum

Basing pre-entry education on capabilities will mean fundamental changes in the curriculum. The current textbook-based, rule-intensive, lecture/problem style should not survive as the primary means of presentation. New methods, both those used in other disciplines and those that are totally new to university education, must be explored. Some of the alternatives for student involvement include seminars, simulations, extended written assignments and case analyses. Creative use of information technology will be essential.

The use of new teaching methods will be a message in itself. Students learn by doing throughout their education much more effectively than they learn from experiencing an isolated course. The skills and knowledge comprising the needed capabilities must be integrated throughout the curriculum. For example, if students are to learn to write well, written assignments must be an important, accepted and natural part of most or all courses. To relegate writing to a single course implies to students that the skill will not be useful throughout their careers and does not require continuing attention. The capabilities must be reinforced throughout the curricular experience.

Teaching methods must also provide opportunities for students to experience the kinds of work patterns that they will encounter in the public accounting profession. As most practice requires working in groups, the curriculum should encourage the use of a team approach.

The development of an efficient curriculum requires attention to integration. Re-engineering the curriculum should include a careful evaluation of topical coverage in all subjects. Emphasis should be placed not only on the presentation of relevant material, but also on the compounding of learning by appropriate combination across course and departmental lines. When knowledge and skills learned early in a university experience are expanded on in work at a later stage, the student's experience is reinforced and enriched.

Faculty

A vital, knowledgeable, creative professoriate is an essential part of the educational process. Most accounting faculty base their course content on information gained through secondary sources—usually textbooks and sometimes standards. They frequently lack other significant, continuing sources of information about the realities of the practice environment. The challenge for the public accounting profession is to assist in developing new ways to maintain a knowledgeable, practice-oriented faculty.

Accounting is a particularly difficult profession in which to maintain a high level of understanding of practice because neither of the two common ways of gaining information about practice is available to accounting faculty. Some professions (for example, most health-related fields) use a clinical model, where faculty are simultaneously practitioners and teachers. Often these faculty treat the most difficult cases or circumstances and thus are not only current in the profession but are also at the "cutting edge" of practice development. At this time, very few accounting faculty are actively involved in practice.

In some professions, much of practice is a matter of public record available to faculty for study and analysis. Law professors may go to their library to find many examples of current practice methods and results. The confidentiality provision for accountants prevents faculty from having access to a robust continuing source of information about the evolution of practice.

The nonclinical, confidential nature of accounting creates a faculty that designs and executes pre-entry professional education without direct knowledge of current practice.

Where other professions enjoy much interaction with their teaching faculty, accounting has a persistent "schism" problem. The classroom experience is diminished by the distance between pedagogical content and practice reality. Academics and practitioners would benefit from the stimulation and challenge that come from a meaningful association.

There is no model for increasing interaction between academics and practitioners in a nonclinical, confidential profession. Current efforts to integrate academicians in the practice include seminars, internships and joint conferences. While these efforts are commendable, a much greater level of activity must be achieved. Innovative methods to increase interaction between the practitioners and the professoriate must be created.

Students
Increases in educational requirements may exacerbate the current trend toward declining enrollments. In the free market of academic major selection, students will have to be convinced that the additional investment is worthwhile. Significant increases in tuition or time must be offset by a stimulating curriculum and the expectation of increased opportunities upon graduation. Efforts to increase educational requirements must also be consistent with the objective of maximizing opportunities for minorities in the profession.

Universities
To achieve a comprehensive re-engineering of the accounting curriculum will require a major effort from faculty. Currently, most institutional reward structures do not attach a high value to curriculum development activities. To ensure the necessary faculty input, individuals must be rewarded for their contributions.

While the responsibility for designing the specifics of the curriculum appropriately rests with the faculty, the role of university administrators cannot be ignored. Without appropriate leadership and support from deans and central administrations, re-engineering of curricula will be impossible.

Accreditation
Accreditation standards have a significant impact on accounting education. At this time, the American Assembly of Collegiate Schools of Business is the sole accrediting agency for college-level schools of business, management and accounting in the United States. The AACSB has recently initiated a major review of the accreditation process.

Accreditation standards must be responsive to the desired outcomes of educational preparation as outlined in this paper. The accreditation process must also be sensitive to, and supportive of, the innovation and experimentation that are inherent in curricular change.

The Opportunity
The challenge for all individuals and organizations concerned with education for the accounting profession is to create a curriculum that will draw the best students and provide them and their instructors with an interesting, demanding and relevant experience. The vitality generated by the creative effort will enrich both universities and the profession. Meeting this challenge will support excellence in education well into the next century.

The opportunity to make the accounting curriculum an active, dynamic experience exists now. A convergence of environmental and institutional factors makes significant change possible and essential. Faculty, universities, accounting firms, professional organizations and accrediting bodies must find a way to work together to create a positive future for the profession.

REFERENCES

Accountemps. 1998. They really like me. *Journal of Accountancy* (September): 14.

Accounting Education Change Commission (AECC). 1989a. *Memorandum of Understanding Between American Accounting Association and Sponsors' Education Task Force.* AECC.

———. 1989b. *Minutes—October 31/November 1, 1989.* Bainbridge Island, WA: AECC.

———. 1990. *Annual Report 1989–90.* Bainbridge Island, WA: AECC.

———, and American Accounting Association (AAA). 1996. *Position and Issues Statements of the Accounting Education Change Commission.* Accounting Education Series, Volume No. 13. Sarasota, FL: American Accounting Association.

Ainsworth, P., editor. 1996. *Introduction to Accounting: An Integrated Approach.* New York, NY: McGraw-Hill.

American Accounting Association (AAA), Committee to Compile a Revised Statement of Educational Policy. 1968. A restatement of matters relating to educational policy. *The Accounting Review* (Supplement): 51–124.

———, Committee on the Future Structure, Content, and Scope of Accounting Education (The Bedford Committee). 1986. Future accounting education: Preparing for the expanding profession. *Issues in Accounting Education* (Spring): 168–195.

———. 1995. *Policies and Procedures Manual.* Sarasota, FL: AAA.

American Institute of Certified Public Accountants (AICPA), Committee on Education and Experience Requirements (The Beamer Committee). 1969. *Report of the Committee on Education and Education Requirements for CPAs.* New York, NY: AICPA.

———, and Gallup Organization. 1991. *Accounting Recruiting Research: Survey of High School and College Students.* New York, NY: AICPA.

Bailey, A. R. 1994. Accounting education: Gradual transition or paradigm shift. *Issues in Accounting Education* (Spring): 1–10.

Barefield, R. M. 1991. A critical view of the AECC and the converging forces of change. *Issues in Accounting Education* (Fall): 305–312.

Barrett, M. J., G. W. Lee, S. P. Roy, and L. Verastigu. 1985. *A Common Body of Professional Knowledge for Internal Auditors: A Research Study.* Altamonte Springs, FL: The Institute of Internal Auditors Research Foundation.

Beaver, W. H. 1992. Challenges in accounting education. *Accounting Horizons* (Fall): 135–144.

Berton, L. 1994. College courses on accounting get poor grade. *Wall Street Journal* (August 12).

Boyd, C. 1995. *A Strategic Education Plan for the 21st Century.* Vancouver, British Columbia: CGA Canada.

Boyer, E. L. 1990. *Scholarship Reconsidered: Priorities for the Professoriate.* Princeton, NJ: The Carnegie Foundation for the Advancement of Teaching.

Brown, C. 1964. Some thoughts on the education of accountants. *NAA Bulletin* (October).

Burton, J. C., and R. J. Sack 1991. Changes in accounting education and changes in accounting practice. *Accounting Horizons* (September): 120–122.

California Society of CPAs. 1995. *The California Core Competency Model for the First Course in Accounting.* Redwood City, CA: California Society of CPAs.

Chironna, J., G. L. Sundem, and D. Z. Williams. 1990. The revolution in accounting education. *Management Accounting* (December): 40–53.

Davis, S. W., and W. R. Sherman. 1994. The Accounting Education Change Commission: A critical perspective. Paper presented at the 1994 National Meeting of the American Accounting Association, New York, NY.

Ehrenreich, K. and R. Hulme. 1992. Evaluation of the AECC. *Accounting Education News, Special Issue* (June): 9.

Elliott, R. K. 1991. Improvements in the early employment experience. *Accounting Horizons* (September): 115–119.

———. 1992. The third wave breaks on the shores of accounting. *Accounting Horizons* (June): 61–85.

————, and P. D. Jacobson. 1992. Bridging the employment expectation gap. *New Accountant* (October): 13–16.

Eskew, R. 1995. Letter to Richard Flaherty. May 3, 1995.

Federation of Schools of Accountancy (FSA), Curriculum Committee. 1982. *Curriculum Guidelines of the Federation of Schools of Accountancy.* Chicago, IL: Federation of Schools of Accountancy.

Flaherty, Richard, ed. 1998. *The Accounting Education Change Commission Grant Experience: A Summary.* Accounting Education Series, Volume No. 14. Sarasota, FL: Accounting Education Change Commission and AAA.

Fox, J. G. 1981. *Knowledge Requirements for Public Accountancy: The Common Body of Knowledge for Government Accountants.* Alexandria, VA: Association of Government Accountants.

Francis, M. C., T. C. Mulder, and J. S. Stark. 1995. *Intentional Learning: A Process for Learning to Learn in the Accounting Curriculum.* Accounting Education Series, Volume 12. Sarasota, FL: AAA.

Frecka, T. J. 1992. *Critical Thinking, Interactive Learning, and Technology: Reaching for Excellence in Business Education.* Chicago, IL: Arthur Andersen & Co.

Gainen, J. and P. Locatelli. 1995. *Assessment for the New Curriculum: A Guide for Professional Accounting Programs.* Accounting Education Series, Volume 11. Sarasota, FL: AAA.

Gifford, W. 1973. Is change necessary? In *Seminar on the Objectives of Introductory Accounting*, 7–13. New York, NY: Price Waterhouse Foundation.

Gordon, R. A., and J. E. Howell. 1959. *Higher Education for Business.* New York, NY: Columbia University Press.

Hulme, R., and K. Ehrenreich. 1994. Accounting education change: Comparison of educators and practitioners. Paper presented at the AAA Western Regional Meeting, Portland, OR.

Institute of Management Accountants (IMA). 1994. Colleges are not adequately preparing accounting graduates for first jobs, say corporate executives. Press release, August 15.

Jensen, R. 1998. Metacognitive concerns in designs and evaluations of computer aided education and training: Are we misleading ourselves about measures of success? Available from World Wide Web: <http: //WWW.Trinity.edu/~rjensen/265wp.htm>.

Kieso, D. E. 1992a. The introduction to "What Colleges Didn't Teach You." *Illinois CPA Society Insight* (December/January): 27.

————. 1992b. Issues from the AECC. *The Accounting Educator* (Spring): 5–7.

Larsen, M. D., and S. S. Ahlstrand. 1991. *Educating Financial Executives.* Morristown, NJ: Financial Executives Research Foundation.

Mathews, M. R. 1994. An examination of the work of the Accounting Education Change Commission. *Accounting Education* (September): 193–204.

Mueller, G. G. 1971. *A New Introduction to Accounting.* New York, NY: Price Waterhouse Foundation.

————. 1995. *Accounting Education Change Commission Progress Report to Sponsors.* June 1. Seattle, WA: AECC.

National Association of Accountants (now Institute of Management Accountants). 1986. *The Common Body of Knowledge for Management Accountants.* Statement of Management Accounting Number 1D. New York, NY: National Association of Accountants.

————. 1988. *Education for Careers in Management Accounting.* Statement of Management Accounting Number 1E. New York, NY: National Association of Accountants.

Needles, B. E., Jr., and M. Powers. 1990. A comparative study of models for accounting education. *Issues in Accounting Education* (Fall): 250–267.

Norgaard, C., and G. L. Sundem. 1991. *Models of Accounting Education.* Bainbridge Island, WA: Accounting Education Change Commission.

Novin, A. M., M. A. Pearson, and S. V. Senge. 1990. Improving the curriculum for aspiring management accountants: The practitioner's point of view. *Journal of Accounting Education* (Fall): 207–224.

O'Connor, M. 1996. Conversation with author. August 13, 1996.

Perspectives on Education: Capabilities for Success in the Accounting Profession *(The White Paper). 1989. Arthur Andersen & Co., Arthur Young, Coopers & Lybrand, Deloitte Haskins & Sells, Ernst & Whinney, Peat Marwick Main & Co., Price Waterhouse, and Touche Ross. New York, NY.*

Pierson, F. C. 1959. *The Education of American Businessmen.* New York, NY: McGraw-Hill.

Pincus, K., L. Scott, J. Searfoss, and C. Clark. 1993. Transitioning for change. Unpublished paper.

Poe, C. D., and J. D. Bushong. 1991. Let's stop pretending all accountants are alike. *Management Accounting* (August): 66–67.

Porter, L. W., and L. E. McKibbi. 1988. *Management Education and Development: Drift or Thrust into the 21st Century.* New York, NY: McGraw-Hill.

Previts, G. J. 1991. Accounting education: The next horizon. *Journal of Accountancy* (August): 35–36.

Richards, J. D. 1992. A conflict of objectives. *Management Accounting* (May): 14–15.

Roy, R. H., and J. H. MacNeill. 1967. *The Common Body of Knowledge for Certified Public Accountants: Horizons for a Profession.* New York, NY: American Institute of Certified Public Accountants.

Schultz, J. J. Jr., ed. 1989. *Reorienting Accounting Education: Reports on the Environment, Professoriate, and Curriculum of Accounting.* Sarasota, FL: AAA.

Siegel, G., and J. E. Sorensen. 1994. *What Corporate America Wants in Entry-Level Accountants* Altamonte Springs, FL: The Institute of Management Accountants.

Smith, R. E., and R. Birney. 1995. *Interactive Financial Accounting.* New York, NY: McGraw-Hill.

Stark, J. S., and M. A. Lowther. 1988. *Strengthening the Ties that Bind.* Report of the Professional Preparation Network, University of Michigan. Ann Arbor, MI: Board of Regents.

Strait, A. M. 1992. Do academic traditions undermine teaching? *The Journal of Accountancy* (September): 69–71.

Stone, D. M., and J. K. Shelley. 1997. Educating for accounting expertise: A field study. *Journal of Accounting Research* (Supplement): 35–61.

Sullivan, M. C., and R. L. Benke, Jr. 1997. Comparing introductory financial accounting textbooks. *Journal of Accounting Education* (Spring): 181–220.

Sundem, G. L. 1991a. Catching up. *New Accountant* (September): 24–28, 59–60.

———. 1991b. Accounting education prepares for the twenty-first century. *Accounting: A Newsletter for Educators*: 1–2.

———. 1991c. Changes in accounting education. *Prentice Hall Accounting Forum* (October): 10–11.

———. 1991d. Changes in accounting education. *Management Accounting Campus Report* (Spring): 1,8.

———, and D. Z. Williams. 1992. Changes in accounting education: Preparing for the twenty-first century. *Accounting Education* (March): 55–61.

———. 1994. Scholarship in four dimensions. *CAmagazine* (April): 39–44.

———. 1995. Accounting educators prepare for the 21st century. *The Irish Accounting Review* (Spring): 157–165.

Williams, D. Z., and G. L. Sundem. 1990. Grants awarded for implementing improvements in accounting education. *Issues in Accounting Education* (Fall): 313–329.

———, and ———. 1991. Additional grants awarded for implementing improvements in accounting education. *Issues in Accounting Education* (Fall): 315–330.

———, and ———. 1992. Ausbildung auf dem gebiet des rechnungswesens. *DBW Die Betriebswirtschaft* (September-October): 595–604.

———. 1992a. Breaking new ground in accounting education. *Today's CPA* (March/April): 39.

———. 1992b. A new age in accounting education. *IMA Campus Report* (Spring): 2, 5.

———. 1992c. Grants awarded to two-year colleges for implementing improvements in accounting education. *Issues in Accounting Education* (Fall): 241–248.

————. 1993. Reforming accounting education. *Journal of Accountancy* (August): 76–82.

Wyer, J. C. 1993. Change where you might least expect it: Accounting education. *Change* (January/February): 12–17.